LET'S GET

Naked

TIFFANY B. LOCKHART

ISBN: 978-1-66784-080-2

Cover Photography: **Allsnap Media, LLC. Franklin Okonta**
Cover Converted by **Halston Shannon Visual Artistry and Branding**
Editing: **Jenny Thelwell – Revolutionary Diamond Publishing Company**
Printed in the United States of America

First Printing, 2020
To find out more information about the author, this book, and other events visit:
www.LGNTiffany.com

My secrets kept me in bondage I was scared they would shame me, but all they did was hold me back.

Welcome to my life.

> "As he came forth of his mother's womb, naked shall he return to go as he came, and shall take nothing of his labour, which he may carry away in his hand."
>
> -Ecclesiastics 5:15 KJV

I don't want to hold on to negativity. I don't want to take anything with me that isn't going to propel me. I just want to walk in my freedom, so naked I shall become; I will share for others to also become naked and walk in their freedom.

LGN.

My secrets kept me in bondage I was scared they would shame me, but all they did was hold me back.

Welcome to my life.

> **"As he came forth of his mother's womb, naked shall he return to go as he came, and shall take nothing of his labour, which he may carry away in his hand."**
> **-Ecclesiastics 5:15 KJV**

I don't want to hold on to negativity. I don't want to take anything with me that isn't going to propel me. I just want to walk in my freedom, so naked I shall become; I will share for others to also become naked and walk in their freedom.

LGN.

I was silent. I was so scared that my secrets were going to come out that I portrayed to be someone else to my family and friends. I withheld myself, allowing fear, doubt, and shame to stop me from walking into my purpose. I let my secrets hold me back from striving to be successful, dream about a business with a big name, or even start a YouTube channel because I didn't want anything I did in my past to be revealed. However, I had to get over myself and understand that everything that happened was for a reason and it was bigger than me. I did not care anymore about anyone knowing of my past and with that attitude, I was to become a force to be reckoned. I decided to let God use me. The saying is pretty real, "whatever happens in the dark comes to the light", BUT if YOU bring it to the light, you have control of how to tell your story and you can manipulate it's trajectory. Take control of your story.

Over the past few years, God has revealed so much to me. I went through a process (and I know I am not the only one who has been here before) that I am now ready to share with the world…in my own words. I want to discuss things that held me back due to my own selfishness, my very own fear to destroy my image. It is time now to let everything out.

As I worked through my mess, I could feel the presence of God with me. He wiped the tears and held my heart as I mended the ugly. I needed His healing hand of all the hurt and pain trapped within. I blamed myself for so many things I went through and I could not let go of the pain.

To heal, you have to go through the process of knowing where you are broken. This may be a tedious process, but it is rewarding in the end.

If you are broken or become broken at any point, you HAVE to go through a process of healing to simply become again. Many times, we say, "man, I just wish things would go back to normal." I used to say the same thing, but I quickly realized you do not become the same person that you once were, which is what I initially thought. I wanted to go back to the old me before everything happened. However, I became a new, stronger person because of what I went through. If we do not heal and go through the process, you will continue a vicious cycle until you learn the lesson. It was time for me to push through for a breakthrough.

Like Uncle Donnie McClurkin said, "For a saint is just a sinner who fell down." I fell down many times, I had to surrender to God and start over again and again.

Just a heads up for all my family members who are about to read this book, everything is A-Okay!

P.S. This is not a blueprint or a step-by-step guide to life. YOUR MAP WILL LOOK DIFFERENT. Mine was messy! I transitioned and overstayed my welcome in many chapters. I was in two chapters (stages) at once and/ or went backward. Although the chapters seem to be chronological, they aren't. Throughout this book, I will be sharing about my mental health, family dynamics, spirituality, relationships, and much more.

I am sharing my testimony through words, songs, prayers, scriptures, therapy tools, and everything else that helped me "become" in hopes that it will help someone else.

Let's Get Naked!

Table of Contents

INTRODUCTION

Insert your full name on the line below.

_____

The first step that I will discuss is getting naked with God, being vulnerable to Him. Take off your layers of clothes. Unravel the true, authentic you. The one who doesn't have to cover everything up; it is a judgment-free zone. God knows every bruise, scar, and scratch that you have. We all have them and although some marks are more visible than others, some are hidden very well. Taking off the façade is the first step to healing and open a relationship with the Father. Once you do this, all of your relationships will improve because you will see the world with different lens. God will heal your scars correctly. The walls fall down, the layers of clothes come off, and now it is just you and God.

I had to unravel the layers of hurt that I held onto for years. Though others may have caused these bruises, it was up to me to fix it and write a new story. The years of hurt and pain became unsurmountable as the walls seemed like they just kept building and overtaking me. People often say, "God will break the door down!" But the truth is, He does not force himself into your life. In Revelation 3:20 the word says, "Behold, I stand at the door and knock. If anyone hears my voice and opens the door, I will come into him and dine with him and he with me."

He knocks, but it has to be your choice to open the door and let him enter; get naked with God.

Chapter **1**:
Layers

. . . .

My Song: Naked – Ella Mai

Your Song(s):

_____

AS A CHILD

I learned how to show people different sides of me. Like many kids, I knew how to behave accordingly depending on who was around or where I was. At home I was loud, funny, and boisterous, but outside of my home I was quiet, shy, and reserved unless there was good ole music, and if daddy was not around of course! However, I was "the angel." I enjoyed being an angel and being wild, I just knew I could not be both at the same time. Every action I took required a secret validation. If I spoke too loudly, I would look around to get a signal from my mom, or other family members. If I asked too many questions and got that "look", I knew I had better be quiet. Everyone complimented and adored the "well-behaved" me. The times when I let my hair down and laughed and kind of just fluttered around like a butterfly, or according to my mom, an ostrich, people would utter. Rude comments and stares as if I was uncivilized; therefore, I chose to keep that side of me within until I got around people would not judge me.

I had lots of ideas, dreams, and suggestions that I shared with family, but they always seemed uninterested. I was full of wonders and I was inquisitive, but often pushed to the side, ignored. Whenever I asked questions, and I did not get a "real", full answer without all the fluff, it frustrated me. Especially if the responses were anything along the lines of: "do as I say", "don't worry about that", or "just don't do it", so I became the type to research for the answers on my own. I was told to stay in a "child's place." Feeling lonely and abandoned, I started to write with hopes that one day I could bring visions and ideas into fruition.

I loved writing and being hands-on with projects. If I could describe my learning style, it would be experimental. I prided myself always on formulating my own opinions. Movies, food, anything people were talking about, I wanted my own to try everything at least once for myself, see the movie, and voice my own review before I listened to what everyone else said. Curiosity really killed the cat for me (insider). One thing I was really curious about at a pretty early age was sex. I lost my virginity at the age of 14 (curiosity killed the cat, there's the insider HA). Sorry, mom and dad. Only some of you caught the joke, and that's okay. I experienced my guilt and shame.

I was interested to know what my friends/siblings/cousins were doing, and why everyone was so into sex. My mom gave me the scary sex talk. She did not give details or examples, she stayed on the surface like church folk do with such topics. "Do not have sex, that is how you get pregnant. Do not be out here kissing because it will lead to sex" which also meant pregnant. I would reassure her that getting pregnant was not on my mind, but apparently having sex was the trend. I could not shake it; sex was on my mind. I knew how to keep other things a secret, I could keep this a secret too if I decided to do it. It was on my mental, but I could not fully ignore my mom's warnings. She made it clear that having sex while young was wrong. Also, the way my family deflected my curiosities about it and their reactions (validation) toward it further confirmed it was something I should not be doing, though not talked about. My younger family members were apparently active and let's just say family reunions were not all fun and games when aunts and uncles would murmur about the "sexcapades" they heard were going on with young kids in the family. I did not want to be the next name coming out of their mouths, so I kept my encounters hidden. I still did not quite understand why it was wrong at the time. It was wrong for teenagers, but right for adults? However, adults had to be married to have sex? But not all of them were married? It was just a bunch of confusion.

But yes! This is how I subconsciously learned what to bring to the light and what to keep in the dark. I simply based on other's reactions. I became a very sneaky and secretive child; I became a mastermind at knowing when to be an angel and when to be wild and I used it all to my advantage. My mom used to say, "Why aren't you like this in school? Around your teachers? Around daddy at home? No one knows how crazy you really are." But even she only knew what I wanted her to see.

THE GOOD GIRL ---
THE CHURCH GIRL

"AW, SHE'S SUCH A GOOD GIRL"

"YOU WOULDN'T DO THAT, YOU'RE TOO MUCH OF A GOOD GIRL"

"I DON'T SEE YOU DOING ANYTHING BAD, YOU LOOK LIKE A GOOD GIRL"

Growing up in a "church family", there were set morals and values were instilled in me from birth. I learned to distinguish "good" from the "bad". I was supposed to know better and there were certain rules I had to live by. I enjoyed going to church because it was the place where I got to see most of my extended family members every Sunday. We dressed up and had so much fun. We went from praise dance practice to choir practice to every single youth event at the church. We would travel from churches in Fort Lauderdale to Miami. On holidays such as Easter and Christmas, and other recognized events such as Black History month, my mom had us present and in the mix. We celebrated Christian-o-ween because in our household Halloween did not exist. Everything I knew about life was from the perspective of the church, my Christian upbringing. So yes, I was proudly a church girl. The church was the most consistent thing in my life until I got to college.

I will admit, although I loved going to church, we all knew how judgmental "church people" were. It was hard to be open to a group of individuals that judged you. This also rubbed me the wrong way and made me shut down, once again controlling what side of me to show them. However, I learned to catch myself when I felt like I was being judgmental or a hypocrite. I mean, we are all human and mistakes are expected, only God can judge.

As previously mentioned, I lost my virginity fairly early and I was not married. I felt so much shame, I broke the rules! I remember sitting in church and hearing the preacher go on and on about not having sex before marriage and it made me feel like less of a person with each word that he said. I knew the difference between feeling condemned by God and being broken down. I felt so ashamed, I just walked to the bathroom and I didn't want to be inside a church again. I felt unworthy and useless. I felt like God was NEVER going to forgive me for that sin. I did not understand why people were not honest about this topic in the church. I knew that if I was internalizing this suffering that others my age must be also.

It seems that the church tries to hide the temptations of the world, weaknesses that one would go through, or even an experience that anyone went through. It seemed to me like EVERYBODY in the church waited to have sex before marriage which was NOT the case. We are all weak at one point and fall short of God's glory. That is in relation to any sin. Church folk had me feeling guilty as heck, feeling like I was the only one who committed a crime and thinking God was shunning me, and sending me straight to Hell. I could not tell anyone how or why I was feeling this way because I wanted to keep my sins a secret.

So, this became the start of a routine. No one had to know about the bad things that I did. My job was to hold on to my good girl image for the whole world to see. Little did I know that all the "bad" that I was holding on to started to become too heavy for me to carry. It was like a huge bag of stones on my back that I could not shake off. My sins were getting stuffed into a closet, and I had no way to release them.

It took me a long time to understand that there is no sin, mistake, mess-up whatever you want to call it, too big or great that God cannot forgive! You were already forgiven a long time ago because Jesus Christ died on the cross, just for us.

THE LIFE OF THE PARTY

I knew how to TURN UP. Everybody knew that about me. I'm getting down as soon as I hear the music. My mother told me I got that from my daddy, and sooner than later I saw exactly what she meant. That man could dance ALL night long. I could not keep up with him and those moves, I do not think anyone could for that matter.

I was a schoolgirl, but I partied harder. I could literally turn up at any event whether it was a party or church. I just enjoyed having fun. By the time I got to college this role was one that everyone got to see and knew me as the "party animal." I didn't hide my wild side anymore; I didn't really care to.

I wasn't ashamed to be on the dance floor. If you saw me, I was most likely to hit my classic wutang dance every time "Naked Hustle" by Ice Berg came on. I was saving the good knees for that specific song.

At the age of 21, I became a drinker and I quickly started to see why I should have never started because my family history with alcoholism wasn't the best. It all happened so fast. I started off hating the taste of alcohol, so instead of not drinking, I took small sips. Next thing I knew I was taking mimosas, peach Bellini's, shots of crown, Cîroc, tequila, Blue juice, Nupe juice, Karl juice, and henny-ritas to the head. Whether I was out with a small crew or a huge crowd, I was drinking. Although, I could be "lit" without the liquor, once I started drinking it was hard to turn down a drink when I went out. I couldn't take one drink and be fine, nope! I can't remember how or when but I started drinking to get wasted every single time.

THE SMART ONE

I felt a lot of pressure with this given title. I would hear it day in and day out about how smart I was, which I didn't think I was that bright to be completely honest, I felt very average with the classes I was taking. I was around very, very intelligent peers to recognize that I was NOT the smartest person in the room, and I was okay with not being on their level AS OF YET. It didn't stop me though because of the confidence my family poured into me. They put me on a pedestal when it came to school. Whenever I went to family events they bragged about my brain, always asked me questions about school, it was the main topic whenever I stepped into the family room. It seemed as if it was already written that I was going to college from day one. I understand now why it was easy for me to accept that I was smart and it is due to the validation that I required to feel "good enough". It was more validating that my grades matched what my family was telling me, I am a smart cookie after all.

I work so hard to truly understand who I am. If you are not firm in your individuality as a person, labels can also come with a portable steering wheel. I had to learn how to overpower my want for validation and take control of my own life without the labels and approvals of others. Although I was proud and happy to be labeled smart, I allowed others to place their personal ambitions over me. Everyone had their own ideas on what a "smart" individual should do. My parents had the biggest amount of control on my steering wheel, (and it didn't help much that I always wanted to make them happy) then there were guidance counselors, friends, teachers, "mentors", and the list went on. Everyone had their voice and opinion on what they felt was the best direction for me to go in. It made it an easy decision for me when the one thing they all had in common was college! I enjoyed school for myself, but I was being built up with the words and labels others placed on me. I chose to go to school because it was a familiar thought for me, it was a comfortable move. I also felt it would give me more time to figure out what I wanted to do. Choosing school was the best choice for me. I can continue to carry the label of "the smart one" and use the time to choose a career of my liking. Note: college is not for everyone, it's okay to fail and try again when finding your own lane in life.

This "smart" label fluctuated a lot. Depending on the teacher and the subject, this label was extremely high or moderate. English and anything that included grammar, writing, and/or reading was a weakness for me. Those grades also came back validating how "not so smart" I was. In high school, the teachers always gave me negative feedback on my essays. It wasn't until college that I actually had a couple of professors who enjoyed my papers or gave credible feedback for my writing. It is actually astonishing that I decided to tell my story through writing after all these years but, God's plan!

AS A STUDENT (STEWART)

I was a hardworking individual and I knew how to work smart and efficient. I believe that everything in life is a lesson, so in every aspect, I was a student. Whether it was community service, working in an office, or in an actual class-room, overall, a student of life.

My ability to shift from good and sneaky played out in everything that I did because simply said, I fed both spirits (characters). I held on very strategically to my good girl image in front of my teachers and supervisors. Yet, knowing that I had a sneaky side, it was easy for me to linger off with bad company. When teachers sent notes home, they usually stated that I was very smart, but very disruptive in class and that I was hanging around the wrong crowd.

Do not be misled: "Bad company corrupts good character."
1 Corinthians 15:33 (NIV)

I straddled the fence between making poor decisions, to impress others, and trying to do what I knew was the right decision. My good decisions such as doing my work and remaining focused in the classroom led me to produce good stewardship, and my poor decisions, such as talking back to my teachers, skipping classes, etc. produced poor stewardship. You reap what you sow.

I had a slick attitude with my teachers. I skipped classes and when I decided to show up, I was a class clown. There was one school year when my assigned seat was on the outside of my class because my teacher wanted to separate me. My parents didn't know I was getting into that much trouble at school because my older brother (or friends) would forge my detention slips. I knew how to get away with a lot of stuff once again relying on my good girl image to fall back on. This was way more dangerous than what was showing on the surface.

I was planting seeds for it to be okay to get involved in bad choices and the more I inched out, the easier it became for me to accept some of my bad behavior to the point that I couldn't tell the difference between what was good and bad anymore. I cussed people out "just enough" where the cussing wasn't too over the top or I would start arguments and fights "just enough" to not get in trouble while justifying my actions with the statement, "I'm a good girl though". That was not true. Right is right and wrong is wrong and there was no in-between. No one is perfect, yet we should strive to feed the right spirit and starve the wrong worldly desire(s) because if you give even a centimeter to it, it'll transform into meters.

Though my brother would help me cover my mishaps, my mother was a fake detective. She sometimes caught me in a handful of bad situations and she gave me the "tighten up" pep talk and laid hands on me (and I am not talking about prayer hands). So, I gladly got my act together for the moment. My parents never personally taught me to be disrespectful or misbehave, I mimicked some of their behaviors to the T *sips tea*, but nevertheless, they corrected me. I was not giving the best representation as a child of my parents to others. In this same connection, neither was I showing the best representation of God in me. Our actions should display who you are led by, if you are one of God's sheep you will know him and his voice.

Scripture Help:

John 10:14 NIV

I am the good shepherd; I know my sheep and my sheep know me

Job 34:4 NIV

Let us discern for ourselves what is right; let us learn together what is good.

Genesis 4:7 NIV

If you do what is right, will you not be accepted? But if you do not do what is right, sin is crouching at your door; it desires to have you, but you must rule over it.

1 John 2:16 NIV

*For everything **in the world**-the lust of the flesh, the lust of the eyes, and the pride of life--- comes not from the Father but **from the world**.*

THE UGLY ONE: SELF-ESTEEM ISSUES

I let others define who I was, how I looked, and how I felt about myself for a long time.

As a child, I was always told I was pretty and beautiful by family members, so it became expected for me to hear those things. From hearing this so much I was confident in my looks. I knew one day I was going to become a model. Every time my aunt would see me she would say, "Ooooooo Tiffany you need to become a model". I had no doubt in my mind she was right and I practiced my runway walk. My very first fashion show was in elementary school. I tripped up and almost fell but my whole family was there to support me, cheering me on, and I kept walking with great confidence. How other people pour into you does matter, but what matters most is what you think of yourself.

Storytime

The story of my low self-esteem begins.

Right about the time children get into middle school is when the hormones start surging and self-image become ever so present. This was true for me. My self-esteem issues really started to kick in at the start of sixth grade. For the first time I heard people outside of my family calling me ugly. "Excuse me, are you talking to me?" I would say astonished at the comment ringing in my ears. This was NEWS to me. I always knew and heard that I was pretty and beautiful. So, it really was a contradiction. Red Alert, Red Alert. What do you mean I'm ugly? The questions began to spiral. Am I ugly? I started to question everything about my appearance. They talked bad about my hair, because I didn't wear weave and they talked about my outfits, which made no sense because we literally wore the same uniform. They argued about who wore it best. I started to consider everything they were saying about me more than what my family members told me. I don't know why, but it just seemed like what my peers were saying was more important to me at the time. It was the "cool" people who had what they called, "dress code" and according to them, I didn't know how to dress, I was lame and ugly in their handbook of life. Whew, what a kick in the face. I always wondered why my appearance mattered so much to other people.

I never cared to talk to anyone about how much their disapproval bothered me. I just pushed through because I figured it was just life. It was normal. This bullying issue seemed very little compared to everything else going on at the time. But their comments really ate me up inside. I held on to them and believed their words every time I looked in the mirror.

My brothers were the ones to pick on me and call me names, that was my normal, that's what my brothers did. So why wasn't I used to it? Why didn't I ignore these kids, like I ignored my brothers? Was it because I wanted these people to like me? My brothers had no choice but to love me. I didn't take their comments to heart and I was programmed to thinking that's how we displayed our love.

The words these kids said to me crushed me and made me a hopeless little middle schooler. I easily accepted their conviction about me and took it as my identity. I tried to change things about myself, to fit in. SOOO EMBARRASS-ING. I couldn't change much though, because, in all honesty, I couldn't afford to dress like them or afford the latest shoes, bags, fancy hairstyles, etc.

Something had to change. I decided to let my guard down a little bit and made some friends. I felt better then, and they didn't judge me by materials. However, the damage was already done and my internal negative thinking had switched from off to on. I'm sure many can recall that one incident that affected and changed your whole view of life, mine happened to be a couple of "bullies" in school that placed me in a long-term battle with an identity crisis.

If anyone thinks they are something when they are not, they deceive themselves. Each one should test their own actions. Then they can take pride in themselves alone, without comparing themselves to someone else.
Galatians 6:3-4 NIV

You know what is cool? To read bible verses at different phases in your life and have a different interpretation every time. When I first read Galatians 6:3, I interpreted it as "don't think you're all that, or above others when you're not" which is the context of the text, meaning do not think that you are too good to not help and restore the next person out of their sin.

But during my healing, as I read the verse, it had a different meaning. God was talking to me through the scripture: "don't think you're ugly when you're not! You are beautiful. If you think you are anything else, you are deceiving your-self!" Bloop. Perspective change. I was in awe.

I was dealing with being called ugly from groups of people I held near and dear to me and strangers. I was too tall, had long feet, a flat butt, and everything else under the sun that was contradicting not only God's words, but also what my parents and family had instilled in me from a child.

I felt like my peers had deceived me and I fell into a trap of deception. I began to play the comparison game. Everyone was better than me. I felt like I was lacking so many things and not appreciating the gifts God has given me. As I was going through my woes, I read the second part of this verse and it put some things in perspective. It read, "Each one should test their own actions; take pride in yourself alone, without comparing yourself to someone else." I took pride in how I was created by God and let go of what others wanted to place on me which was not of God. I thanked God for that interpretation.

AS A FRIEND

I strived to be a loyal friend and I thought that meant saying yes to a lot of things. I figured it meant to always be there whenever they called or needed help. I felt such a responsibility that even when I couldn't be there, I had to stay on the phone and always go the extra mile for my friends. I sacrificed myself to be "loyal" because I didn't want to lose any of them as a friend nor did I want them to think I didn't care. So, I was driving myself crazy and stretching myself very thin trying to be there for everyone.

As a close friend, I spoke my mind a little too much. As a distant friend, I kept my thoughts to myself more often. I understood everyone couldn't handle my honesty, although some others desired and needed it. I had to learn when to speak up and when to shut up. I needed to understand discernment. These relationships were very important to me.

I didn't like losing people, but surely through friendship I learned this was also a part of life. The friendships I kept allowed me to become more compassionate and trusting. Everyone does not enter to stay through every season of your life. This was a hard pill to swallow. I was a people pleaser and I tried to do everything to avoid being disliked, abandoned, or left; but of course, I learned I couldn't please everyone. I had to let go of some of the people who were not meant to continue to travel life with me. However, I never fail to still congratulate from a distance and support from a distance. I am so thankful for the many friendships and the valuable life lessons they taught me.

We need friends, it is not good for us to always be alone. We need others, we simply cannot get through life alone. It is one of the very reasons why God created Eve. She was placed on the Earth for Adam because it was not good for man to be alone. If we are alone, who will God use to correct us or teach us?

As Iron sharpens iron, so one person sharpens another.

Proverbs 27:17 NIV

Who is shaping you to be a better version of yourself?

_____

_____

_____

_____

How do you define a friend?

_____

_____

_____

_____

How do you define an associate?

_____

_____

_____

_____

Describe your friends in your inner circle.

_____

_____

Do your friendships push you or hold you back? How so?

_____

_____

_____

_____

What is your foundation of friendship? Values? Standards?

_____

_____

_____

What is your level of trust for these individuals? Rate 1-10.

_____

Are you vulnerable together?

_____

_____

_____

Do they correct you? Do you correct them?

_____

_____

_____

Do two walk together unless they have agreed to do so?

Amos 3:3

At some point, two people who were total strangers began to call each other friends. They exchange phone numbers, get to know each other better, and they meet up for good times. They extend the relationship from stranger to something more. At this point, the relationship is meaningful and both ensure to help each other grow and which makes it a transactional relationship. Just make sure that you both call each other friend.

The foundation of your friendships matter, but also the building, transforming, keeping up with, and maybe even demoting from friends to associates is important.

As a friend and associate, it was natural for me to cheer, push, give advice, and provide motivation. I strived to keep God at the center of everything that I did even when it came to my friendships. I learned how to treat my friends because of my friendship with God, I kept God as an example of how we should treat people we love. It was easier to be my authentic self with others who shared in my beliefs. It was not that I didn't associate with others, but I could clearly distinguish who I called my friends and who were my associates due to my values and belief systems. Note: Being an associate to someone is NOT a bad thing. To be honest, I think about how much money and time I save by having more associates than friends.

LETTER TO MY FRIENDS

Song: Girl - Destiny's Child

October 9, 2019.

I don't like the spirit of jealousy to take over my heart. I am bluntly announcing to you both to forgive me of any jealousy. The reality of the situation is to point it out and clean it out, so it doesn't have a hold over me. I love how smart, funny, and determined we are as individuals. Sometimes jealousy comes upon me when I compare myself to others (vulnerability). I am asking God for a clean heart. I am asking for forgiveness from him and you as well. I don't want anything to hold me back from becoming everything God has intended me to be.

I can remember always judging and comparing myself to empowered women which was not healthy. I want to be more empowering and uplifting and motivational when I see you doing great work. Cheering you on always! I declare that jealousy will no longer be a natural thought of this circle. Uplift, motivates, and pushes. When I see the good work, I will ask if there's anything I can do to help or ask how I can also attain that instead of wondering how you did that. I believe doing this will not only show how inspired I am by you, but it will also help me eliminate the jealousy and the asking of "why not me."

Cleaning my heart, love you ladies.

Sincerely Tipp and God #100percentME

The message above was sent to two of my closest friends to express how my jealousy was trying to break apart our friendship and if I hadn't recognized it and been on this spiritual journey, I would have allowed it. It was hard to recognize my jealousy and come to terms with it. I had to go to war with it and confront the jealousy that lived in my heart. Some will let evil stir up on the inside of their hearts, thinking there is no way you could feel such a way about your own friend, sibling, spouse, or whoever. But it is very possible. Many times it is not intentional. I had to put an end to my jealousy by confessing and cleaning my heart out. Due to my foundation of God, He showed me things that were not of Him and affecting many of the relationships that I was involved in. My jealousy toward others, once confronted, became motivation. This meant I became more inspired by watching the great things happening with them instead of having evil jealousy.

THE ONLY GIRL

In my nuclear family, I was the only girl. I had three older brothers and one younger brother. I knew what it felt like to be a sister, a younger sibling, and an older sibling. However, I personally did not get the opportunity to learn how to share my space with other girls/ women. I only had myself to worry about. Everyone had their assumptions on what it was like being the only girl, "I know you were spoiled" "that must've been rough living with all boys" "I feel bad for your future boyfriend" and many other sayings.

Yet for me, I was proud telling people I had four brothers with my whole chest sticking out. My brothers spoiled me and treated me like a punching bag all in one. I learned how to take the hits, I learned how to take the cracks and not fold in front of people, but rather I covered up and pushed through. My brothers along with my father taught me how to have tough skin when I needed it most, which also resulted in holding in my feelings. I'll never forget my father's favorite saying, "stop crying like a 2-year old" which I feel like he's been saying since I was 2 years old, but I learned how to suck those tears right up.

As the only girl, I felt a lot of pressure to be the "do-the-right-thing" child. It was normal in my upbringing that boys got away with much more dirt than girls. They were catered to more if they messed up, given a pass, or a slap on the wrist while girls were more bashed and expected to know better. I hated the double standard. One very popular example of this was cheering for the boys if they were to have sex at a young age, but for the girls it was the total opposite. We were talked down upon and the boys got a high five. Like really, what is that?

My brothers got away with so much just because they were boys. They got away with not cleaning and they got to go out with friends whenever they wanted. It was so hard for me to get out because I had to take more caution being a girl. I received less freedom; my life was more controlled and geared to making sure school was first for me.

The comparisons between me and my older brother were crazy, especially when it came to school. A piece of the sky would fall off if I were to get bad grades and/or get in trouble at school. I had to hide whenever I did get in trouble. The lectures were always different, "you know better, don't do it again" versus my brother's dry "Do Better" speech that he would receive which my parents just grew tired of saying. The expectations were weighed differently. I would hear my parents say continuously that my brothers were smart there was just always a "but" after it that would contradict everything they just said. Instead of being firm and just saying, he's smart. This created the balance scale for how each child should act and what they could get away with.

AS A DAUGHTER
Song: Perform - Travis Greene

I admittingly struggled with people-pleasing but, in this role, I was a people pleaser to the 100th percent! It didn't matter how much I disagreed with my parents, I couldn't stomach seeing them sad, upset, nor disappointed for long. I strived to make my parents proud. Since a little girl, I wanted to be everything they wanted me to be to keep a smile on their face. I noticed how my brother(s) stressed them out, so I honestly didn't want to be the child who did that. My actions and reactions to my parents enabled a lot of their behavior to set high expectations for me.

I wanted to make something of myself so that my parents could talk about me to their friends, cliché, I know, but their faces lit up as they bragged and that was my goal at the time.

I liked dancing, but I did it more so for my mom because it made her happy when she came to see me perform. I participated in flag football and basketball to involve myself in something that maybe my father would come out to see. I tried a lot of things to ensure their happiness.

As a child I soaked things up like a sponge. I have a very vivid memory of what my parent's relationship was like. I always noticed how stressed out they were arguing with one another. I just wanted to see both of them happy and I thought I could be the one to do it. It became my role: the one to keep them happy! It may sound ignorant reading it now, but as a child, this made so much sense.

I did not want to be one more thing they had to worry about. Whenever I saw them arguing or frustrated, I would wait until they were done arguing to step in and do a sweet gesture or kind act. Sometimes those kind acts meant getting good grades to bring back home, cleaning the house, or giving a hug/ kiss. But even though I did these things, it didn't change anything. The arguing happened so much, that sometimes I would just daydream about what my life would be like if certain things were different. I mainly thought about how my life would be if my father were someone else and if my mother remarried another man. What would it be like if my father remarried and I had a stepmother? I began to think I was the worse child in the entire world because I wanted my parents to get a divorce so bad. I prayed to God to fix it so they did not have to argue anymore, and if that meant a divorce, then so be it. If someone else can make them happy, I was fine with that (I know right, "it be your own kids.") Some-times it felt like I was praying for their downfall. Sorry. I really just wanted the arguments to stop. It constructed my whole view on marriage and what love looked like. I did not want anything to do with marriage if it resulted in arguing like my parents. I always thought about my wedding day, but my mother and father made me second guess how "long" I wanted my marriage to last every other day. I thought maybe I had to go through few marriages before I could enjoy it. Let's get naked.

As a daughter, I could not be perfect. As a daughter, I could not be everyone's example to follow. As a daughter I made mistakes. As a daughter, I didn't know better. As a daughter I became a husband to my mother, and angry at my father.

STRATEGIC PLACEMENT FOR AN UNIQUE PERSONALITY.

We are all strategically placed in this world. We are unique. Not one person is the same as the next person.

Just as I felt I knew myself; God knows me even better. I was strategically placed in my family, to be born at a specific time, to go through these struggles to mold me into who God needed me to be. I was a perfectionist, when I want something done, I want it to be close to perfect. I pay attention to details. I am a challenger; I push myself and others around me. I'm hard-headed, I have a slick mouth. I'm lazy sometimes. Some of my values include family, loyalty, justice, respect, and equality for the big and little things in life. I could've started a debate team and created new laws to fight against why my brothers shouldn't touch food in the fridge that did not belong to them (hahaha). I like organization and order. I enjoy roles and labels, clarity and understandings. Communication is a big interest of mine. My beliefs, my adversities, and my triumphs have shaped my being and is connected to my unique purpose on this Earth.

And we know that in all things God works for the good of those who have been called according to His purpose.
Romans 8:28 NIV

WHO AM I?

I went through the process of listing out of all of these labels and roles of myself to get you here. In each of these areas, people-pleasing was one thing in common with every layer. I cared more about how others saw me than my own internal views. I had to give up people-pleasing if I wanted to live my life for me…for God. Once again, I couldn't please everybody.

In this moment are you able to answer these questions: (if not, that is okay)

Who are you?

_____

_____

_____

_____

_____

Which labels have you or others created to make up your characteristics to be the person that you are today?

_____

_____

_____

_____

_____

Song: Finally Found - Travis Greene

I grew tired of going up and down on the rollercoaster, trying multiple resources, school included to figure out my identity and purpose in life. After trying everything else, I found myself on my knees and talking to God, telling him who I was. Well, who I thought I was and I was ashamed. I felt worthless, useless to the world. I felt like a broken individual who couldn't get fixed, nor could I do anything right. Nothing could fill this void, regardless of the number of accomplishments I made, the external situations going on, internally I did not feel good about myself.

Everything that I was pouring out to Him was how I truly felt about myself. I really had to look in the mirror and be honest. I put all the fakeness aside and how I wanted other people to see me.

I jotted down how I really felt about myself versus what I wanted others to see.

How I felt internally:	How I want others to see me:
Ugly	Beautiful
Sad	Happy
Depressed	Full
Empty	Whole
Like Trash	Confident
Unworthy	Pure
Broken	Easy-going
Like A burden	Successful

For you:

How I feel internally:	How I want others to see me:

For a moment I would like you to go back to the "Who Am I" questions. Really sit and think about some of the things that others told you about yourself, those things that you feel stuck in defining who you are. For example, my family always called me smart, they used me to tutor and help everyone with their homework. I placed smart in the category to define who I was because I heard it over and over. However, we know that everything we hear is not all sunshine and rainbows. I was always made fun of because of my body shape, the jokes were funny no doubt, but I always thought something was wrong with my figure because of it, that became a part of my identity because I also heard it continuously.

I hit a pivot point in my life when I just decided I am not going to carry it anymore. I'm going to let it go. All of it. Everything that anyone ever said about me that was used to tear me down. I knew that I was fearfully and wonderfully made by God's image, but it was hard to believe this statement if I carried around the labels that others placed on me. I wanted to use what God said about me as my identity instead.

Prayer:

Dear Heavenly Father, I come before you to ask for forgiveness of any sins I have created, known and unknown, before I ask for anything dealing with your favor. I just want to say, Thank you for your grace AND mercy. Now, I begin to ask:

God, how do you see me? Your identity for me is the only one that matters.

When you receive your answer, place them in your God's Labels chart. You can come back as the spirit of God reveals to you throughout the day, week(s), or month(s). I listed a few scriptures for assistance, Listen to God through his word. (Personal decision to create more boxes on a blank paper if needed.)

GOD'S LABELS

Scripture Help: **Psalms 139:14 NIV**	My thoughts: **You created me in your image.**	God's labels: **Fearfully and wonderfully made.**
Scripture Help: **Genesis 1:27-31 NIV**	Your thoughts:	God's labels:
Scripture Help: **Psalms 139:13-17 NIV**	Your thoughts:	God's labels:
Scripture Help: **Jeremiah 29:11 ESV**	Your thoughts:	God's labels:
Scripture Help: **1 Peter 2:9 NIV**	Your thoughts:	God's labels:
Personal Scripture:	Your thoughts:	God's labels:
Personal Scripture:	Your thoughts:	God's labels:
Personal Scripture:	Your thoughts:	God's labels:

REWRITE YOUR NAME HERE (In Capital Letters): _____

_____

Song: You Know My Name – Tasha Cobbs

The only way that I could really get naked was if I stripped away all the labels that others placed on me and started to listen to God's definition of who I was. It was hard to break down and unravel who I thought I was because it was 20 plus years of training and experience. It was normal to me, it was how I started to function, so creating a change was the hard part. God's identity for me brought me feelings of freedom, openness, and acceptance. I could care less about meeting other's expectations.

I am accepted by God; I am chosen by God. I am different. God reminded me of who and whose I was because I definitely lost sight. Everything started in my secret place with God.

Chapter 2:
Product Of My Environment

· ·

My Song: Bag Lady – Erykah Badu

Your Song(s):

_____

We all learned a lot about how life should be from somewhere or somebody. However, at some point we must take off our "borrowed" clothes and put on our own. We must dig deep to our foundation by peeling off the layers one by one. The clothing that my parents (and family members) gave me which were life lessons I should adhere to in order to become successful not always rang true for me. All habits, all behaviors, all moral and ethical values taught to me were not all correct, but they worked for me growing up. I had to unlearn some of these foundational virtues and create new ones. In this chapter I dug deep and navigated all of the crevices of my upbringing to give you a true experience of the complexities of my life in this chapter.

Notes:

- There is always room for change.
- What you learn/learned can stay or go. Your choice.
- No one lives the same life; you are unique. Therefore, we all see the world differently. You can try your best to help others see your world's perspective, but they may not understand it and that's okay.
- Everyone doesn't speak your dialect, even if we all speak English. We all grew up differently.

NOW BEFORE YOU'RE LIKE, "OMG YOUR PARENTS TAUGHT YOU THAT?", THIS INCLUDES WHAT I WATCHED AND ABSORBED FROM MY ENVIRONMENT GROWING UP. THINGS THAT I LEARNED INTENTIONALLY AND UNINTENTIONALLY.

I thank God for the parents he gave me because they were a part of this mission. Even when we did not see eye to eye or became very frustrated with one another, they were who I needed. Although I am mature and more open minded now, I did not have the same attitude of gratitude growing up. My fast lips helped me receive many beatings, yet I tried my best to honor my parents, respect them, and apologize when I felt I was wrong. Through it all, I know for a fact that they loved me unconditionally.

PARENTS

Both of my parents come from an African American background. My father's family is from Georgia and My mother's family is from Alabama. Each of my parents have huge families. Therefore, their upbringing, the time frame of when they were born, and where played a huge role in how they raised me and my siblings. My father was the second to last born of his mother's children and my mother was the oldest child in her nuclear family. Both were born in the '60s. They were equipped with survival tools and knowledge that they passed on to me, yet in that same breath, I am equipped with many different tools than what they had. This is mostly due to the change and evolution in society. The world was much different when they were growing up in comparison to my upbringing. For example, I am more likely to quickly send an email, rather than sending a letter in the mail as they are better at doing.

My parents took pride in showing me how they were raised to chase the bag. It was in their everyday language as they told me repeatedly to ensure I go to college and save money. As my father would say: "Money makes the world go around" and "make sure you are saving your money". Being in their household they spoke long enough for me to recognize their daily thought process. Clearly I could see my father's mind was always on the money. His focus was making sure that we had a roof over our heads and food to eat.

My mother would drill into my head, "Make sure you find a job with benefits and start saving in a 401k." I would hear her consistent stories about having multiple jobs at an early age while going to school and providing for the family. My mother wanted me to be set when it was time for me to retire. Although she was a little more outgoing when it came to traveling and exploring life outside of everyday life, than my dad. She struggled yet had faith that money would not be an issue. She enjoyed life with restrictions due to finances and she didn't want the same for me. We were all living in financial bondage.

The stress of money started with my parents and it trickled down to me. I worried about money all the time. When I wanted to go out with friends, my first reaction was to check my account even if I had just gotten paid. I was constantly battling a decision on whether to spend money on food or leave it alone in my "emergency" fund. I always feared that I would run out of money. Though my tactics would be viewed by most as being responsible, the issue was that it gave me anxiety. I adopted my parent's worries and it was hard to break that cycle until I stepped out on faith and saw that God continued to provide every single time. I had to TEST my faith to TRUST my faith.

I wanted more out of life. I wanted to be able to experience financial freedom. It seemed like the culture for every black family in my environment was similar. My experience: work hard to get a college degree, then work hard to get a good paying job, then work hard to earn for retirement. If times got rough, guess what, WORK HARDER! The plan was to work as hard as you can until retirement. Once retired, then you can rest and play. I didn't want that type of life. Many people retire and then get sick and never really get to enjoy the fruit of their labor. I just know I wanted a different outcome, so I had to pivot my sense of direction. I had to figure out a new path, new habits, and develop friendships with people who had the outcome that I wanted, which unfortunately were doing the total opposite of what my parents had taught me. It was heartbreaking yet it was true that I did not want to end up like my parents. I pushed to create a new path. It wouldn't make sense for me to stay in the same mindset, and on the same path with new information. Someone once said, "Do what you can until you know better, then do better." I had to pour my new "wine" (knowledge) into new "wineskins" (person) (**Mark 2:22 NIV**).

While I was living with my parents I hoped and wished they would think about changing or see things from my point of view sometimes, but they were fixed in their own ways. It's what they knew and what had worked for them while growing up. It's what they had learned in their environment. My mother was a little lenient and listened to my ideas with an open ear sometimes. I was grateful to have her support from time to time.

At times I felt like an outsider. I had developed a different mindset and it pulled me further and further away from the people I loved the most. I was going after what I wanted in life and there was nothing anyone can say or do about it. I wanted to do multiple things and being stuck in a box wasn't one of them.

My college experience expanded my thinking! I was introduced to a diverse group of individuals who challenged my way of thinking and even the way I was brought up. Here I was trying to hold on to the values and beliefs I had been taught my whole life but also agreeing with this new way of thinking. I didn't quite like the feeling, but I was open to it. I decided I was going to show them my way of doing life, instead of pushing it on them.

I had to take a leap of faith to leave my house and implement this new mindset that was going to help me reach my goal.

I graduated from college learning about so much more than book work; it was a whole life experience. I knew that I had outgrown the environment I had at home. It was so obvious after graduation that I was not the same 17-year-old when I left for college. I had matured in all aspects. My mind, body, and spirit did not fit into the same space. I felt myself going backwards and getting complacent. Everything was annoying me. Going to school, taking orders from my parents, my brother needing me, and lastly, I had no privacy and I was done! I was aggravated to the tenth power because I just expected much more out of life now. I got the "post-grad" depressive symptoms because I knew there was more to life than this. It sucked that the reality of the situation was that the opportunities available for a young, black professional female was still very few in my community. It is the same environment that had me stuck in my close-minded thinking. I couldn't go back to that. I applied for work in other areas, got an offer and jumped at the first opportunity to leave.

"MA"

She was my role model. I wanted to be just like my mom: hard-working, strong-minded, and always getting things done. My mom is a smart woman. She's great at math, she could kill a crossword puzzle, and she plays a lot of Scramble, so I figure she has a big vocabulary too.

My mother is a devoted Christian, a prayer warrior, and an open worshipper. She is always doing something for the upkeeping of the church, continuously reading the word, all the while working for God. She is a very caring and supportive individual who is always ready to help the next person. She's the type of person who is present at every event to show support. Whether it is buying products, calling to check up, or just to show support, she is present. She carries her motherly spirit around everyone she knows and is willing to provide and protect as if you were her own family. Though she has many great qualities, my mother was controlling. She always felt she was right and was the queen of trash-talking to my dad. However, she knew how to apologize when she was wrong. She was the matriarch of the family. She wanted to make sure everyone was set because otherwise she would worry herself to the maximum. She wanted us to be safe and feared any negative outcome. She always made it happen and provided for me and my brothers whenever I needed anything. She portrayed leadership attributes, a willingness to learn and plan, and enjoyed making others feel special. The list on how much she does for her family and others is ever going.

Values, positive characteristics, and morals were splendid virtues the matriarch instill in me and my brothers. She tried to refrain from sharing her past experiences because it wasn't a path she wanted me to follow. She neglected the fact that in not sharing, she left the opportunity for me to make some of the same mistakes. I ended up staring the same battles she did right in the eyes. The only way I got to hear those stories were by digging and pulling out information from family and friends or stumbling upon old pictures. Every once in a blue moon, Ma would tell stories about fighting her ex-boyfriends and those were funny. But any who! She never mentioned things like getting drunk or sex before marriage, but I did my research on her lol! Once I found out some of the things my mom had gone through, I really didn't feel as bad or ashamed about my own sins. I was kind of relieved.

One trait that my mother pushed heavy, was for me to have a willing spirit to do for everyone as she did when she was my age. These were large shoes to fill. Truth be told, I didn't want to fill them. My mom did for so many people that she would neglect caring for her own needs. I thought this made her like a superwoman who could do anything and be there for everyone, except herself. Though I didn't want to necessarily follow her footsteps in that capacity, I couldn't help my big heart. I started going down the same road, but as I aged it was not something I necessarily admired as much, because I knew that I couldn't become so involved that I forget about myself. I sat and watched my mother's health decline due to trying to be there for everyone else. I understood the principle of compassion, giving, and doing for others as the Christian way of life, but you also have to feed and care for your own body to continue this process (**Ephesians 5:29 NIV**). You cannot do anything fully, on an empty cup. Self-care matters.

LIVING FEARFULLY

Mommy always had a sense of worry and stress about her children. She wanted to know that we were safe and protected, which was classified as normal motherly tendencies; "she's only worrying because she's your mom and that's what mothers do" they said. My mother almost always placed her fears, doubts, and worries on me. Whenever I sought out to do something or plan to go somewhere there was support, but along came statements of doubt. "That may not work." "Don't travel too far." Comments she made sometimes sparked fear in my decision-making process.

It is usually the person closest to us that can have such an impact on our decisions. We tend to listen to these people because we feel they want the best for us.

We want confirmation from them in order to move forward with our own ideas. "Oh yes! This way has to be the right way!" because my mom or my pastor, or my brother, father, whoever said so! You fill in the blank with who you received confirmation from; but the truth is, everyone is different and what may ring "right" for one person, can be wrong for another. We all see life from a different **lens** depending on our life experiences and the vision that God has given to us. This is why we cannot take on someone else's truth or purpose.

In spite of negative comments, I always walked into a conversation or situation confidently, even if I knew my mom was going to have something negative to say. I had to protect my confidence at all times before coming to her to share my dreams. This is my truth, and I'm speaking on it. She had a worrying mindset and feared more about what could go wrong. I never liked her putting that in the atmosphere for me. I loved the support, but I could honestly live without the negative commentary. So, if that meant taking away the need for "support" then I just had to live with it. I usually came to her when things were in its final stages and I had proof that everything was going the way it needed to. But that still didn't stop my dear mother from finding something else to worry about.

I can recall a time when I was applying for colleges and there was one school I really wanted to go to, but there was some negative news in the media about it about an incident that had occurred on that campus. She sent me the article. It read, "Black person lynched in …" and you know what came next, right? " I don't think it is a good fit for you to go to school there." She constantly brought it up to the point I didn't even want to apply to the college anymore, and I didn't. This is one of many instances where I allowed fear to take over my life decisions. **Sidebar:** I thought the match of my parents was funny because my dad never really provided the mental support, but he didn't doubt that I would get it done. He would just say, "Make it come true." On the other hand, my mom provided all the support, knew I could do it but feared and worried throughout the process of me getting it done.

I had a bad habit of listening to others and neglecting to hear God's voice. I tended to lean on the guidance of people who I thought had my best interest at heart. Being able to finally Hear God gave me the answers I needed. Don't think that the people closest to you, may not be feeding you information that is not aligned with God's word. Not that the information may sound bad, or foolish, because it can appear to be good, but not the advice that you need. They also may not be intentional on giving out this "not needed" advice, but nonetheless, its impactful. My mother gave great advice however, she did not always have the "right" answer specifically for me. It was a hard pill to swallow because I leaned on her the most for guidance.

Finally, I shifted gears and made God my source for guidance before coming to anyone else for answers. In His true nature, I was directed to bible verses, sermons, and people He intentionally placed on my path specifically for me. I knew they were God sent because they lined up with his vision and kept me on track. I listened and respected my mom's insight, but I also had to decipher which parts to not feed too much into because some of her answers and decisions stemmed from worry and fear and that alone does not come from God. Yes, we should keep watch for what is going on around us, to be prepared; yet, do not live fearfully and get stuck being afraid. I am protected and covered by God and I stood firmly in that belief. I always told her don't worry, God got me. With God, I did not worry because I knew my body and mind are always at ease protected by Him.

Scripture Help:

Psalms 118:6 (KJV)

The Lord is on my side; I will not fear: what can man do unto me?

Psalms 46:1-2 (KJV)

God is our refuge and strength, a very present help in trouble. Therefore, will not we fear, though the earth be removed, and though the mountains be carried into the midst of the sea;

Joshua 1:9 (KJV)

Have I not commanded you? Be strong and courageous. Do not be afraid; do not be discouraged, for the Lord your God will be with you wherever you go.

Deuteronomy 31:6 (NIV)

Be strong and courageous. Do not be afraid or terrified because of them, for the Lord your God goes with you; he will never leave you nor forsake you.

LIFE STAGES AND DISTANT RELATIONS

My mother thrived on solving issues. She may go through feelings of worry and stress before she gets to problem solving, but she was indeed a problem solver. She tried her best to fix any wrongdoing. She never wanted to see any of her children sad, angry, or hurting in any way, and if we were, we didn't have to worry about asking for help, she was already brainstorming. As a child this type of behavior was very needed because we couldn't do certain things on our own. However, helping us with every little difficulty as an adult can be more of a hinderance to us. Sometimes, we have to learn how to get ourselves out of our own mess.

Just naturally whenever I was in trouble my mother was the first person I called. I leaned and depended on her so much. However, at some point our relationship became uncomfortable, and we began to clash quickly. We didn't know how to transition from the stage of needing all of her help, to only needing some of her help. She didn't know how to take a step back so I can take the step forward to figure out life on my own. We argued frequently and the older I was getting the more I wanted to watch and learn how she did life and not her "doing" life for me. I wanted her advice to help me get through problems, not solve them for me.

Her problem-solving mentality and me knowing that I could run to her for everything started to inhibit my growth in different areas of life as a young adult. I would get mad when she tried to help me do something that I was really trying to do on my own. I wanted her to show me and then I try but it usually resulted in her taking over the entire situation and doing it all herself. I hated being treated like a baby. I felt very unprepared for the world and it made me angry. On the other hand, I felt guilty for taking any anger out on her when she was just trying to help. I didn't know how to make her understand that even though I appreciated her, I wanted to handle my problems. I began to distance myself from her and to minimize going to her for help. After a while, she noticed and inquired. At the time I didn't even know how to verbalize my feelings to her in fear of hurting her feelings. However, it felt so freeing to finally move on the situation how I wanted. I learned to solve my own issues without running to mommy. I eventually found a way to include her in my life without making it overbearing. I found that asking for advice via phone instead of asking in person made a difference. It allowed us to speak more because she didn't have immediate access to me to take action. It worked so well because it fulfilled both of our needs. She still felt needed and I still managed to have control over my own situation. We were transitioning in the "family life cycle" which is just a fancy name to describe the changes and stages in a family, as the family members age over time. We started to rekindle and grow our relationship into the stage of parent and young adult (the launching center stage). This was important to learn to do in a parent to young-adult child relationship because I believe my mother and I over-extended our time in the parent to school-aged child stage.

SUPERWOMAN

As I aged, my starry eyes when I looked at my mother disappeared, and I knew reality had begun to sink in. The curtain over my eyes were lifted and I no longer saw her as a superhero. She was human after all. She taught me that it was okay to not be strong all the time because we all get weak at some point or another and it is totally normal.

Life has a way of showing us who we are, especially at critical times when we don't expect it. My mom got into an unfortunate accident suddenly, she became physically unstable. The accident affected her health causing her to not be as a mobile as she used to, and I felt so guilty. There was nothing I could do to help because I was away in college and even worse, I am the one who asked her to go to the place where the accident happened. I felt like all of this was my fault. I traveled to see every chance I got and would even select classes near my home so I could continue to visit. Unfortunately, it became impossible juggling work, school, and campus involvement with all the traveling. I was trying to be responsible with my college career while mind-handling the guilt of what was happening at home. My mom always reminded me to just have fun at school, and not worry but that did not stop me from thinking how she was struggling at home and at work with simple everyday tasks. Although my mom was assuring me everything was okay, my aunt would call and say otherwise. I was worried to say the least. Other family members also called to pressure me into doing more for my mom. I was between a rock and a hard place.

My mother pushed hard for me to focus on school and did not want to interrupt my education while I was away at school. However, when I stepped foot into my household, I would be fair game! She had a to-do list ready for me with places she wanted me to take her and other chores I needed to help with while I was there. Mommy was not the type to ask, she just assigned you to something and told you about it later. I hated that. She never considered that maybe I had something planned. Year after year, she did the same thing. I got a to do list soon as I stepped foot in the door from college. In a way, I was proud that she felt she could count on me to get errands done without feeling like a burden to other people. I just wanted her to understand that I needed time to myself too. She would continuously say, "I can't wait until you move back home." The roles had switched, and my mother became dependent on me.

I noticed how my mother's sickness was taking a toll on her mentally and physically and I can tell she felt defeated by it. She grew tired of asking people to do things for her and became frustrated at those who she expected to do things for her (me included) whenever we would have an excuse not to help. Her sickness made her feel like a burden.

By the time I graduated and moved back in, my mom had already accepted and grew comfortable with her new way of living. There went to physical therapy sessions, doctor visits, had multiple prescriptions, and unfortunately the inability to drive and travel as freely was her new normal. ·

Though she had accepted this new way of life, I couldn't help but want more for her. I wanted her to fight harder. I wanted her to be strong and not settle. I placed my expectations on her. I was trying to push her to do more to get her to overcome this stupid sickness. I wanted her to fight for her freedom to drive herself wherever she wanted to go again and to practice washing her own hair again. I just didn't want to see her give in to this way of life. She didn't see it my way though. We got into a heated argument because I felt like she was settling with letting people do everything for her when I never knew her to be that person. I felt like she lost her faith in getting healed and got comfortable with doing less. She let this sickness become her identity. I didn't see my mom as my role model, my superhero anymore. In my truth, as usual my expectations dug me into a hole. I was mad at my mom for accepting this and not pushing through like she always did before. I didn't want to be like her anymore. In this reflection, I only got hit with a harsh reality, I am not my mother. I would not have folded like she did if it were me in her situation. I guess I set too high of expectations and too much pressure on her. I realized I was at fault for all of the arguments. Not everyone needs a coach. I also imposed my personal expectations on her. Once I got rid of my expectations, I was able to accept her for who she had become which was someone who was simply trying her best. She was still a caring, devoted mother, sister, daughter, friend, and wife trying her best. She was going at her own pace, and her own rules with what life gave her. She was the expert of her own life.

Her Shoes Didn't Fit

12:07 PM.

My mother's shoes don't fit.

I tried and tried to push my feet in, it was not working.

At one point they were too big

And then they were too loose

Then as I got further into the closet, her shoes became too small

And then they were too tight.

I wanted to be like my mom

But my life was not supposed to be a replication of hers

I was supposed to do something different

That's why.......

My mother's shoes didn't fit.

UNSPOKEN CONVERSATIONS VS. SPOKEN CONVERSATIONS

Misunderstandings. Lack of communication. Parentification. Despised Roles. Burdens. Anger. Tiredness.

My mother and I carried each other's burden without speaking on them. It had been four years of avoiding and ignoring our problems. Unspoken conversations resulted in a lot of yelling, crying, and screaming then sometimes an apology afterwards.

"I'm tired of this! You never ask if I'm busy, you just assign me to tasks. You come to me to do things for you, before you even ask your own husband!"

"I don't have anyone else to do it for me!" "I'm sorry that I'm such a burden!"

I was relieved and fearful all at the same time. On one end I got to release anger but I couldn't take the process of holding it all in to explode in conversations like this. On the other end I feared raising my voice at my mother, flinching backwards because I thought she might slap the black off of me but I couldn't keep quiet anymore.

Previously I have described at times where my mom and I did not see eye to eye because we did not express or communicate our emotions, this is the story of when I fought to speak up to my mother on a more sensitive topic. There was a major pivot in our relationship.

Story Time

I shared my feelings of anxiety to my mom.

I wanted to be more open with her and let her in on what I was dealing with. I didn't want to keep it a secret anymore and go through it alone and I really wanted her support. Anxiety is not an illness that others can detect easily so, I wanted to explain to her what it was. One day we were sitting in her room and I started to have a panic attack. I tried to take deep breaths, relax my mind, and slow down, but the thoughts would not stop. I kept gasping for air, but I felt like the world was closing in on me fast. My mom was sitting across from me on the computer. She didn't realize I was experiencing a panic attack, so I waited to calm down before I said anything to her.

I finally got up and put away my racing thoughts about how she would respond and built up the confidence to tell my mother about this issue. I said, "Ma, I think I have anxiety". She responded, "What kind of anxiety do you think you have?" I thought to myself, "whewww what a relief, she's interested in learning." I started to give her information about anxiety and then she proceeded with a response that could possibly solve my problem. It made me happy to hear it. I was ecstatic because mommy's response showed me how much she cared. Before I knew it, she had an ongoing list with solutions to my anxiety.

Most were valid and some I had heard before, but I honestly did not want a problem solver. I just wanted her help, differently. I wanted her to LISTEN. I wanted her to understand what I was going through. I wanted her to hear me out. I wanted empathy, but all I got were solutions. She was so ready to fix me like I was a project.

I appreciated my mother's attempt to help, but I made all my wants and expectations of how "I" wanted my mom to react overpower my emotions, and this caused me to speak less on the situation at hand. I could've said how I felt at the moment like, "hey mom, I know you really want to help, but I just need someone to listen right now." Instead I continued speaking going deeper and telling her my personal experiences with anxiety. I thought that would give her a hint. She yelled, "WOW, Nesh look your school's football team just beat that team!" my hopes were crushed and void, AGAIN. LOL.

Now the devil would have got a kick out of letting me play my mom's response over and over in my head because all I saw was her going back and forth from the computer to her phone while I explained one of the biggest issues of my life. I thought about this moment over and over in my head on how I would tell her about my issue only to find out I'm really just talking to myself because she's preoccupied with nonsense… yay! Now, note that this is not the first time I have important conversations with her and this has happened. This is why I refrained from telling my mom things in the past and preferred to deal with issues on my own.

I couldn't believe that it happened AGAIN, and as much as I wanted to be mad, I couldn't. I just walked away. I had to express my issues with someone else who would listen to my anxious thoughts now.

The only difference this time around with Ma was that I decided not to hold a grudge against her that would last days without telling her why I was mad. I decided to go back to my mother (two days later, yeah, I know) and discuss that it bothered me that she did not give me her full attention as I was sharing an important dilemma I was experiencing. She understood, apologized and also advised me to speak on what's bothering me earlier next time so that it does not stir in my spirit. She had a valid point. I, too, apologized.

This one conversation patched up an argument that could have lasted weeks due to my stubbornness which could've resulted in a shift in my mom's perspective as a parent. I asked her if she could put the phone away and just hear me out next time and that opened the door to a "listening to understand" conversation. It was exactly what I wanted. Sometimes it doesn't always work out the first time, or the second or third time but then we create expectations for others and get upset when they don't meet them. Everyone is wired differently and most importantly; we will make mistakes. My mother was not trained to be a "therapist", so I couldn't hold her responsible for not responding like one. We both had to put work in to create a difference in how we wanted to communicate. I had to put my pride aside, resist holding a grudge, and tell her what upset me. She had to put in effort to listen. It was a two-way street, and I am glad we both were willing to work on it. Be patient in your relationships with others. Communicate effectively. Listen attentively. P.s. everything that my mother did in this conversation, I also did unto others, I had to unlearn this behavior.

To the spirit of fear, that causes my anxiety I speak:

***In the multitude of my thoughts within
me thy comforts delight my soul.***
Psalms 94:19 KJV

46

Cast all your anxiety on him because he cares for you. Be alert and of sober mind. Your enemy the devil prowls around like a roaring lion looking for someone to devour. Resist him, standing firm in faith, because you know that the family of believers throughout the world is undergoing the same kind of sufferings.
1 Peter 5:7-9 NIV

Meditate on your mind, as I learned through a podcast, the speaker Sarai T. said: don't let your mind become the devil's workshop; but I did my own remix and continuously said to myself, "my mind is NOT a playground for the devil."

KEEP AND DELETE

There is always something that we could learn from people and our encounters with them. In any relationship, there is a transaction. Hang around others long enough and you will surely start to flock together, mimicking each other's behavior and catch phrases. Your personalities will start to blend.

I wanted to be intentional and hold myself accountable for what I desired to learn or unlearn from my parents, that would work specifically for how I wanted to live my life. A big chunk of my parent's personalities was present within me. For me to correct and change some of my behaviors, I designed a "keep and delete" list. By doing this I could recognize some of the things that I did subconsciously just like them. My list started off very short because I was prideful in thinking some things weren't "that bad" or didn't need to be changed. If I talked about any of their faults, I was also pointing out my own (which was the point, right? LOL). Mockers resent correction, so they avoid the wise (Proverbs 15:13 NIV). Acknowledge. Unlearn. Correct. Practice. Mess up. Forgive. Correct. Practice. Your choice.

There is space provided for you to write down your own personal "Keep and Delete" list to add what you want to keep from your parental figures (if you want to keep or delete anything) and you can also add what you want for yourself. List how you envision your best self to be. Just remember to be honest.

My Mother (figure) taught me:

KEEP	DELETE
Praying everything in Jesus name	How to worry about everything
How to Worship	To answer every phone call
To verbally apologize	Trash-talking my dad
Participate in community service	Lack self-care
To be caring and supportive	Panicking over little things
To verbally say I love you	Talking to people while doing something else
To be a good friend	Being a hoarder
To clean up after yourself	No boundaries
To always say thank you	Spending a paycheck before it comes

My Father (figure) taught me:

KEEP	DELETE
Discipline	Usage of cuss words
To say no	To not verbally apologize
Apologize with action	Not hold me accountable
To be organized	Lying
Self-care	Pride
Hard work	Say whatever I want, however I want
To be a giver	Disrespect my mother
Independency	Disregarding other's feelings
To rest	To settle

For you:

My Mother (figure) taught me:

KEEP	DELETE

For you:

My Father (figure) taught me:

KEEP	DELETE

"DAD"

My Song: Never Call Me - Jhenè Aiko

I always felt like daddy's little girl even when I disliked some of my father's actions. He spoiled me like a princess, what can I say? I fell victim into forgiving him and standing up for his actions many times because he was my dad. My father spoiled me the best way he knew how, with food and personal gifts. My mother and my brothers knew I could get my dad to say 'yes' to some things that he would turn them down for, so technically they would send me in as a weapon. As my oldest brother, BJ, would say, "I can do no wrong in daddy's eyes."

From my perspective, Daddy was a working man, always out and about. His schedule was the same every day. He went to work at 4 am, came home to take a nap from 12-2pm, and headed back out of the house to hang. I felt like my father was very distant and barely around for household family functions. Anyone who came to my house knew that my daddy was not a home body. I remember people asking, if my dad lived with me and asking if my parents are still married because they never saw Daddy.

My relationship with my father was somewhat rocky because even though I knew how I felt about him, I could not ignore his absence in our home. I struggled with being "daddy's little girl" and recognizing Daddy's faults. To me, Daddy was a comedian, a dancer, a chef, a disciplinarian, a protector, and a provider. However, I also noticed other characteristics that he showed more towards my mother and others which included being verbally aggressive, prideful, manipulative, and a liar. I rarely received this treatment, but I also found ways to avoid those type of outcomes with Daddy. I spoke to him indirectly as to not upset him and when I had any issues, I would tread lightly because I knew how he would react. I tried my best to always remain in the daddy's little girl role and seldomly did we step out of that relationship.

My father is always ready to preach to someone. He had lectures for days. He has a lot of wisdom; however, it was very hard to listen to the knowledge he gave sometimes because of his actions. He didn't always practice what he preached. My father always had a story to share, but he wouldn't share them with me. I was jealous about that. I always saw him sitting and talking to everyone else. Most of our conversations weren't long or in depth growing up, unless it were me and my brothers sitting on the couch getting an infamous 10-hour lecture because one of us got in trouble. Other than that, it was back to regular, we said hello and checked in with each other whenever I was home from school.

Daddy and I spoke one day, and he told me about an idea he had about a sitcom. I was excited that he was having a conversation with me. I was grateful that he wanted to talk and share his ideas with me. We talked about how sometimes dreams must get pushed to the side when you want to provide for your family, but that we should never lose focus of them. He gave an example about a young lady that started making movies from her iPhone. She shot the scenes, edited them, and added the final touches all on her phone. She found a way to make her dreams come true even though she had a child to look after and now she is a movie producer. I think it all was just a lecture for me because he reminded me at the end that I needed to stay focused and on track. Overall, I was just ecstatic about having a regular conversation with my daddy and it made my heart jump for joy. I was an emotional rollercoaster when it came to my daddy. All I ever wanted was his **attention**.

ABANDONMENT

As a child I didn't understand the many decision adults made. I can remember wondering why daddy was leaving the house every day. At the time, I did not even think that these decisions were for the betterment of the family or even just for me. It seemed like everything was black and white, yes or no. No explanations or details just decide and move on it while us kids just stood around being pulled in each direction.

I knew that daddy would leave the house every day early in the morning and return in the afternoon. After a while I started to realize that even when daddy had a choice to stay at home, he wouldn't. I started to feel abandoned by Daddy. I looked at everything from an abandonment perspective and I internalized these actions and blamed myself for not being enough and for him not choosing me over wherever he was going. Abandonment.

I did not have the answers to why my father chose to leave the house all the time. I would ask questions hoping to get answers, "daddy, where you are going?" He would respond, "oh I have to go up the street or step out for a little while. I'll be back." I got used to him always leaving the house.

I could not help but think that my dad wanted to be anywhere but at our house. I began to make up my own stories in my head. I came up with scenarios, that made sense to me. Hmmm, maybe he has another family? I'm sure that might sound absurd to some people, but I was a child who constantly witnessed my parents arguing and I also watched a lot of movies lol. That was the only thing that made sense in my head. My dad did not want to be around this family because he had another family, a "better" family.

I really wanted to spend time with my father more than anything, but my thought process and creating many assumptions from unanswered questions, the feelings of abandonment just kept resurfacing. As I got older this issue grew with me. Every time I chose to spend a weekend at home, the feelings of abandonment resurfaced. The environment made me feel so yucky inside. I soon realized the root of most of my problems came from home.

You see as I got older and these issues trickled into my adulthood, it burdened the relationships I was in. In my romantic relationships when my boyfriend would leave my presence, I felt abandoned. I felt like he was leaving to see another woman like I used to think Daddy would do. IT WAS NO LONGER A CHILDHOOD PROBLEM. Going off to college did not fix the abandonment issue I felt by Daddy, it only provided a break from the pain.

When I was home, I felt the pain repeatedly. I really thought I was over it, but there I was back to crying myself to sleep, crying in the shower, wishing my father were different. I didn't understand why I was still having these feelings of abandonment. I thought I was okay, even when my father was reaching out more, and giving more effort to build a better relationship, I still felt this abandonment. Immediately I realized that I ran from the problem, but **I never healed**. The triggers remained the same. I only thought I healed because I didn't live in that household anymore. Out of sight out of mind, right? Exactly.

I couldn't understand why the enemy was after putting that image in my head and wanting to keep my relationship with my father at a tear. But I was fighting for it, for that same reason to not give the enemy the joy of breaking up my family and fighting through my abandonment issues.

I went through years of the roller coaster abandonment issues, holding on to decisions that my father made when I was younger when it came to my mom and our family. Holding this against my father, and every other male I dealt with. I viewed God as a father figure as well, I placed the same abandonment issues I felt from my biological father on God. I had to break the chain.

COMMUNICATING WITH MY FATHER

At times I would try to approach my father, but I had a habit of stuttering like I was a toddler because I feared upsetting him. Most times I would open my mouth only to realize no words uttered out of it. I treaded lightly because I knew if whatever I said to him made him angry, he would yell, walk away while I was still talking, or simply would not care to listen and shut down the whole conversation. His way or the highway. After all, he was the parent and I was the child, right?

I wished I could talk to Daddy like I do with my mom. I was more expressive with her because I felt she understood me more. She was a bit more sensitive and it made her easier to talk to. I was able to communicate, scream, cry, pout and let out my emotions to be heard. I couldn't do this with my daddy because at some point the conversation always seemed to backfire on me, and I would be the one getting the consequence for saying how I felt. I tried explaining to Daddy that it was hard for me to open up to him sometimes and that's why I always communicated with my Ma more. I was afraid and I didn't want him to become the person to me, that I saw him be with everyone else when discussions didn't go his way. He was like night and day.

I had a lot of problems with communicating my feelings to Daddy and even though I wanted to bite the bullet and I was afraid that if he denied his actions, I would totally shut him out. I hated when people did not hold themselves accountable for their actions. I've witnessed him before throw an issue right back in the face of the other person and not acknowledge his mistakes in the matter. He behaved this way all the time. I just let Daddy's actions ride for a long time and the fact that now I couldn't get my point across to him frustrated me tremendously. Even though I noticed his actions since a child, I couldn't be the one to "check" Daddy because I had to stay in a child's place. I wondered why he didn't know better. Why was it that he never apologizes when he hurt other's feelings? Yet, everyone gave him slack and said, "that's just your daddy." So, I shrugged a lot of things off.

COMPARISONS AND EXPECTATIONS: UNSPOKEN CONVERSATIONS

Ma made countless efforts to get Daddy to show up for his children at events or any important function, but unfortunately it put more emphasis on the fact that Daddy did not want to be there. We would see and hear Ma blowing up on him over the phone, forcing, and yelling at him to get in place. My brother and I got the picture early. It also showed in most of the photographs we took because we could see that it was just us and our mom in most of the pictures.

I begin to compare my dad to other dads I saw at dance recitals, games, and other events. It hurt that I had to beg Daddy to be at something that I felt was important to me. I gave up on that, I told him the date and time, I figured if he wanted to be there, he would come. I put up a defense mechanism (repeatedly) so that it wouldn't hurt me as much when he didn't show up. I made myself believe that I just didn't care anymore.

To make matters worse, I was influenced by sitcoms and compared "tv" dads to my daddy. I also listened to songs like "Dance with my Father" by Luther Vandross to set expectations for my relationship with my dad, making me feel even worse about the reality of my situation with Daddy. I expected him to be like these individuals and when he wasn't holding up to this standard of a father, of course I was crushed. My comparisons and expectations damaged the relationship more than what it already was.

If you guys still have not picked up on this mistake yet, I'm saying it again, I had to let go of these high expectations I placed on others. Furthermore, as my high school teacher always stated, "when you assume, it spells out that you make an "ass" out of "u" and "me". I did not speak to my father about what I wanted to see from him. I just assumed he would do it. I felt like he should've known, after all he was the parent! I expected him to be like the father I saw in other families and on television without me telling him. It was a backwards way of thinking (I see that now). How can anyone change if they do not feel like they are doing anything wrong? I didn't tell Daddy what I needed from him and he couldn't read my mind. I just accepted that treatment from my dad, not caring to speak up because I didn't expect him to change. He didn't listen to my mom when she brought it to his attention, why would he listen to a child?

As I got older, my built-up emotions spiraled out of control and everything he did agitated me more and more. I hated when people told me not to feel how I was feeling. Don't tell me to just be grateful that my dad is still around and be grateful he is working to provide a home for me. You are telling me to completely disregard the way I feel and push my emotions off to the side like they are not important and don't matter. I felt both, grateful and hurt!

Don't tell me that I'm too old to feel this pain. Don't tell me to just get over it, you don't think I tried that? You can't run from your feelings forever. You have to address the root cause and address it or else it will haunt you forever.

After becoming immune to hearing people tell me to be grateful and get over it, I became conditioned and started to say this to myself and others, "you shouldn't cry over this, that's nothing to cry about." Then I would realize that I hated when people told it to me!!! So, I started to tell them yes, you feel how you want to feel. I'm not in your shoes. I would not be able to understand that feeling. I would want them to explain it to me so that I could hear them out and let them know that their feelings are valid.

When my father broke promises, wasn't true to his word, or even simply left the house all day, no one ever taught me how to mend the pain that I felt they just told me to shake it off. Broken promises led to low expectations. If Daddy told me we're going to do something together or take me somewhere, I didn't really have much hope that he would follow through. I shook it off, that was life. I was told I didn't have to be mad or sad about it. I leeched on to other's feelings instead of comforting my own. I was told there would be another time, then "another time" came and nothing changed. No one gave an explanation, no one comforted me, no one called Daddy out on his missed promises. I wish I had spoken to Daddy about my issues sooner than later, because it took me a long time to heal from these wounds and feel comfortable around him again.

I believe that feeling this pain helped me become an advocate for my niece. She came to me as an 8-year old expressing her issues with abandonment and neglect from (my brother) her father, yes at the age of 8. I thought I was look-ing in the mirror at myself. I understood her pain and decided to break the chain. First, I asked her if she wanted to voice her issues to her father, she said yes but she was nervous, that's where I stepped in. I personally wanted them to speak about her issues face to face because no one ever gave me the opportunity to do it with my own father. I understood my feelings as a child, feeling abandonment and not being able to speak up to my father about it. I decided I wasn't going to ignore her problems or try to give her my opinions about the situation, instead we were going to the source. I set up a mini intervention for my brother and niece. I was there as her advocate, so she could feel comfortable expressing herself openly also I didn't want my brother to lead the conversation and overpower her because she was the child, this was her conversation that she was leading to him.

I had high hopes that this would break something between my brother and his daughter's relationship. Although I had no one do it for me, I wanted to be able to do it for someone else. For a very long time I was looking to fill this void of daddy issues in the wrong places.

My unspoken conversations usually filled up the pages in one of my many diaries/journals/ phone notes, excuse my 'French' but I decided to let this one out:

11:20 AM.
People THOUGHT I should've been happy because I was so "spoiled", and they THOUGHT I was the happiest girl in the world.

Well NEWS FLASH, I DIDN'T CARE ABOUT THE F*CKING MATERIALS THAT I GOT!! THE REASON BEHIND ME GETTING THE MATERIALS WAS USUALLY A JUSTIFIED MAKE-UP GIFT, TO FILL THE VOID ABOUT NOT BEING THERE! SO, I AM F*CKING PISSED EVERYTIME I COME HOME BECAUSE I'M TRIGGERED AND EVERYONE WANTS TO DOWNGRADE MY FEELINGS. NO ONE UNDERSTANDS WHY I DON'T WANT TO BE HOME. YES, I WANT TO BE WITH MY FAMILY BUT I CARE ABOUT MY MENTAL HEALTH AS WELL. I CAN'T CONTROL MY FEELINGS SO, "F" ALL OF IT!

Song: Emotional Rollercoaster – Vivian Green

10:42 PM.

My feelings were always dismissed.

It was feeling like I had to be grateful because I was told to. I latched onto their feelings about Daddy instead of my own. I never got to deal with my feelings because I redirected my feelings to what everyone else told me to feel. Therefore, I dealt with their emotions and not mine. My feelings were still being held within and once they began to resurface, I pushed them down over and over again and repeated the process of latching on to what others told me to feel. So, the betrayal and hurt that I wanted to feel about my dad when he broke promises or didn't stand on his word, kept ringing true. I didn't let those feelings play out to deal with them, understand them. I overpowered them with gratefulness that I had a father who was still in my life, like they said I should. I was being thankful that I had a father who could provide for me, and I pushed away those feelings of abandonment, that he also provided when he wasn't there or even when he was home and still was not present with us. I pushed down the thoughts of feeling hurt and the fact that they made me cry because I WANTED a relationship with Daddy, but I knew if I cried then he would tell me to stop whining like a two-year-old. I never got to deal with the fact that I didn't have to be perfect to please my father all the time because I latched on to the idea that well, "at least he came to 30 minutes of your game" so when he was there I had to give it my best because I didn't know how long he would stay.

I literally, signed up for activities with my dad in mind, just to get him to come out. I figured he didn't like the dancing and cheerleading thing, so I tried out for basketball and flag football. I didn't get to deal with the fact that I shouldn't internalize my father's actions. What he did was what he wanted to do, and I had no control over it, but I didn't know how to deal with that as a child. I put all the blame on myself because I ignored my true feelings. I had rather latched on to feeling grateful and happy, because the feelings of dislike, hate, and discomfort didn't make me feel good, but in the end avoiding all my feelings only made things worse because I needed to fix the problem and no longer stick a band-aid on it.

(I had to restructure my thinking. Eventually, I learned my lesson and began doing things for me.)

YOU DON'T KNOW ME

Daddy should know me for the simple fact that he is my dad. No other require-ments necessary. The lie detector determined that was a lie. Ha! Getting to know someone takes curiosity, interest, and effort. I truly believed that Daddy missed those characteristics. Maybe he just didn't care to know who I really was. Because this became my thought process, I gave up putting in the effort for the relationship that I so much desired to have. I felt like I didn't need to continue beating a dead horse. He barely called or texted to communicate. Therefore, neither did I. I became one of those people that called only when necessary. It was easy to live this way since I was away in college anyway.

When I finally spoke up about my Daddy issues, it wasn't even planned. I didn't have anything specific to say in mind and I was scared to sound reckless. Even worse, I spoke out loud and everyone heard me. I said what I felt on my heart, I cried, but most importantly I felt heard. I blurted out all my feelings in a room full of my SISTUHS, an organization I joined in my undergraduate years of college. I was grateful for their support at such a time. I was able to unleash what was still bothering me after all these years. No matter how big and bad I thought I was or how much I pushed it away, I couldn't deny how deep this issue cut me. I would've wanted this moment to play out differently though. Many times, I thought about asking Daddy to a lunch date so that I can discuss what was bothering me, but I was afraid he would refuse. I didn't think my ego could take it and so I didn't ask to avoid rejection and abandonment. Besides, I wanted to talk about more than just issues, I wanted to build a father-daugh-ter relationship. We didn't know each other beyond the surface. We knew just simple things like each other's favorite foods, him going to work, me going to school, our hobbies, his- the racetrack, mine- dancing. I felt as if my father had no idea who I was and vice versa. He didn't know certain things like what I was allergic to and it seemed like he never remembered my birthday and I was always confused on his. It was just like whatever.

I wanted more from him, but I didn't care to force him to change. I just prayed about it and left it alone. However, God kept reminding me to not give up, even if just a little chat here and there. It was not an easy task for me, I threw in the towel every single time my efforts weren't reciprocated. The more time went on, the harder it became because I was really trying to figure out why I was the one leading the flow of this relationship?

I really wanted Daddy to put in the effort. Why didn't he want me? Why didn't he care enough to mend and build a relationship with me, his ONLY daughter! Once again, I had to let go of my expectations. I just accepted the little he gave and moved on. If he called or texted, I was happy to hear from him. If I didn't hear from him, that was cool too. I had to take on this type of attitude because it was affecting my mental health. I wanted to let go feelings of unworthiness, like I wasn't enough for him. I love my father, but I had to let go to heal from the disappointment of our relationship.

SPOKEN CONVERSATIONS

I had to go through a lot of healing and speaking with my heavenly father in prayer to get the feelings of anger and bitterness out of my heart.

Forgiveness was very hard to even think about, because for me, that required an open dialogue with family, and we were not the talking type of family. Who was I to change that? Someone who needed answers, that's who! The dynamics of my family had to change. I was very anxious and afraid to start calling out people who were wrong about certain situations or how they behaved toward each other (me included). I did not know if my family was going to accept the challenge of change. I thought it would break my family up if they didn't take it well.

Fear prolonged me from having spoken conversations and I was afraid of talking to my dad in general because he was very easily aggravated. Apologizing and "sorry" wasn't used much in our household and that meant that we would have to talk about the situation again. However, I can say that we were better at showing our apologies through actions. Whether it was making someone a sandwich or giving up your last fruit snack that was how we showed we were "sorry". It was very normalized in our home. (However, my mom was raised differently. My mom's family was filled with strong-minded women and they were confrontational. Everyone spoke up about their feelings at some point, but they too struggled to be listened to because they argued more than talked. I wasn't a big fan on that strategy either. Overall, I got stuck with not apologizing, or not talking about it at all and just letting it blow over.

One day though, I finally said the words, "Daddy I forgive you" and I thought my heart would automatically be healed. I was waiting for the moment for everything to feel lighter in my body. You know like they talk about when giving testimonials in church. LOL. I was waiting for the light to hit me or something. But I didn't feel anything because I was struck with shock. Daddy's response left me in a trance. He blamed me! I found myself even more upset and angry, downright dismayed!!!

When dealing with forgiveness there is always two sides to the story and usually neither party necessarily feel like they are in the wrong. We are not wired to think that it was our fault. We like to blame others for the way we react in a certain situation. Apologizing was not our response. We didn't want to accept that we hurt the next person. So, we avoided apologies and disregarded the other person's feelings because that would mean that we're the "bad guy." Face it, who wants to be the bad guy? Not I.

However, I had to move beyond that way of thinking, and I began to verbally apologize to people more. It made me feel different. I became more compassionate and vulnerable. It allowed me to be less prideful. I got to step outside of myself and apologize for my shortcomings and even just apologizing if I made a person feel a certain way.

After the incident, Daddy cooked me breakfast and we sat and watched a show. I knew what he was doing. As usual, we act like we're sorry by actions, and not with words hoping it will it blow over. I decided that I would write a letter and it read:

09/14/2018

Letter to my father:

Dear Dad,

I am sorry for telling you that I didn't remember all of the happy moments we had. It was not meant to come out that way. But I just wanted to let you see my perspective of everything because I was hurt for so long. I can tell that hurt you, I am sorry. I felt like you went to go cry (I don't know) when you left in the truck, but I don't know, because when you came back you were doing that little thinking thing that you do on the porch. But from my view whenever I invited you to something it was a 50/50 chance that you would show up. But I held on strongly to that 50% that you would show up. When I asked mommy if you were at a recital, a performance or event, the amount of times she said "no" was hurtful, I felt like you never chose me. Yes, boys could do that, they could leave, choose other girls all these things but you were my dad. And I just felt like it was supposed to be different with you. I just wanted you to choose to be with me. So, on top of boys treating me this way, it felt like my own dad was doing the same. And I felt very worthless. However, I love you and I am ready to work on our relationship.

P.s. I do remember one of my favorite memories, when you would take us to Boomers, and I would always be scared of the wooden roller coaster, but you made me feel safe.

RESUME:

After writing out a bit more of my feelings, I felt relieved. I finally felt that weight that everyone spoke about come off my shoulders. I was glad that this time I could get all of my emotions out and not be interrupted or cut off and getting my words deflected. I got it all out on paper with no judgement or fear. I actually forgave him without even saying it to him this time. I had the opportunity to release on paper. At that point it really was more about getting it all out, rather than wanting to feel the forgiveness, or worrying about how my father responded. I held on to feelings of abandonment and unworthiness for so long, that the release was tangled in between letting my real feelings out to the person who I wanted to hear it the most, my dad.

The letter was me forgiving Daddy for myself, a release. I knew Daddy wasn't able to do so at the moment because we just didn't have that type of communication and honestly, I don't think we knew how to communicate with each other. That night he told my little brother to tell me thank you for the card. Lol.

The good, the bad and the ugly.

HE'S _MY_ FATHER

My father loved me, he always called me sweetheart or sweetie. He cracked jokes, he would fart and make me laugh. He made me my favorite breakfast on Saturdays. He was only a phone call away when I had car troubles. Though I wanted him to fix the car, he talked me through the steps over the phone to fix it if he wasn't able to come to my rescue. My father taught me how to be independent. Daddy had a sweet place for me because I was his favorite girl, he always told me that. I believed him, but I needed his actions to match.

My Father Never "Cared"

My father never cared to come to my recitals

He never cared to come to any of my games

My father never cared what my favorite food was, he made sure I ate all of my vege-
tables.

My father never cared to say I love you,

My father showed he loved me.

My father never cared if he gave me the last of his cash,

My father never cared if I was crying

He went to find something to make me happy

My father never failed to make me breakfast every Saturday.

My father never cared to put me in the latest clothes or shoes.

My father never cared about the little things,

My father protected and provided.

My father never cared to let me believe the lies of this world, he never cared to hurt
me with the truth.

He told me, "ALL THAT GLITTERS ISN'T GOLD"

My father is MY FATHER.

I stop putting such an emphasis on all the negative and looked for more positives.

MY ENVIRONMENT

After being away in college, I went back for 3 weeks and of course I recognized every trigger different this time as soon as it happened. I didn't understand why I may have been triggered when it first happened, but I did understand that my mood and feelings were changing when certain things occurred. I was able to piece things together and it just made more sense now.

It was sign of healing, but I wanted to pinpoint exactly what I was healing from. Was it my abandonment issues, my toxic relationships with my exes, childhood trauma, and my feelings of self-hate? Was it just one of these things, or was I healing from it all, all at once? I wanted to leave and run away so bad. I was so mad, so hurt, so frustrated. I blacked out and had anxiety attacks. Once again, an emotional wreck, but I couldn't heal correctly until I broke everything at its root.

When my childhood issues came to stare me in my face, I chose to seek therapy to help me heal from that trauma. I didn't want to hold on to my issues any longer. My problems were holding me back and I wanted to get a handle on them. In a perfect world, I did want my parents to hold some type of accountability and notice their part in some of my trauma. But it didn't even matter, at this point, I was in therapy for me. My parents taught me all they knew. The good and the bad (subconsciously) to shape and mold me into the person I am today.

I think it's important to watch carefully for what ideas and interests you gain from your living environment.

PRODUCT OF GOD

As it may seem hard to decipher what your parents want for you and what God wants for you. God places things in our imagination as a child that He will always take us back to.

I know many parents feel they know what's best for their child, BUT remember we are all God's children. Take a step back and make room for God's ideas. It is important to pour into these ideas before placing labels on who you want your child to be (speaking now or futuristically). I believe the same Holy Spirit who guides me, also guides everyone else, parents included! The spirit gives discernment, corrects your ways, and allows you to lead and follow God's way. Parents make mistakes and so do children.

> ***Every good and perfect gift is from above, coming down from the Father of the heavenly lights, who does not change like shifting shadows.***
> **James 1:17 NIV**

In relationship to the parent (figure) and the child you both are a gift to each other from God. He's been strategic since before you were born. The "why" will reveal itself sooner than later.

Take this time to jot down and listen to what creative, child-like thoughts God may be reminding you of right now. Child-like meaning without the knowledge that you have now, as if you were a child who knew nothing. Listen without inputting the visions, plans, and dreams that you previously established for your life without God; listening now may save you a lot of time. However, it is not too late to go after this either no matter how old you are.

These thoughts may have been there since the beginning of time, something you always wanted to do and never listened to or stumbled away from because of other's opinions. Don't think about what others have planned and placed for you to do. Meditate on God, wait. Put the phone down, put the book down and just listen.

Dear God, please reveal to your children what it is that YOU declared for them to do.

Proverbs 19: 21 NIV – Many are the plans in a person's heart, but it is the Lord's purpose that prevails.

Child-like Thoughts:

Chapter 3:

Trusting Him?
Trusting Him.

My Song: Focus – H.E.R.

Your Song(s):

_____

Different trials and errors in relationships that allowed my trust to fail in all areas, until I trusted and focused on HIM (GOD).

Now, I will break this down and show you how my romantic relationships intertwined with the relationship I had with my biological father, and eventually led to an increase in serious relationship with my spiritual father, God. It is key to note who you are, who you are in relation with others, and why you are that way. You will start to notice connections, similarities, differences, and self-reflections. This chapter is all about my continuous fails at relationships, digging from the wrong well!

MY FATHER, "MY FIRST LOVE"

Whenever anyone chose me whether it was a friendship or relationship, I tried my best to remain loyal because I knew what it was like to feel abandoned. Yet, whenever someone chose me to be their friend or girlfriend, it also felt like a treasure to be chosen. So, I wanted to hold onto them even if it didn't mean they would hold on to me.

My first love taught me how to be spoiled, so I didn't care when boys tried to show off "flashy" things. My first love taught me how to be treated nicely. I learned how to hold myself up as a beautiful queen. My first love taught me how to serve and do for others. I loved to do for others in my relationships. My first love taught me how to seek outwardly for attention, instead of feeling like enough from within.

The one thing I failed miserably at was wanting male attention. So, when I got it, it was like "wowwwwww, what is this?" *cues heart eyes* I'm in love; end of story. I had to learn to heal my abandonment wound, strategically for when males showed me attention, I could grasp the attention but not be blinded by it, I still had to see pass the B.S. A special thank you to my first love.

RELATIONSHIPS
Song: Good to Me – H.E.R.

For the sake of my personal opinion, I will not list the time frame of my relationships. Just enjoy the ride!

In each relationship it seemed as if I always made it out just in time. It's like something in me still knew that I deserved better. Even though I sat in the situation for a while, my mind slowly exited out of it. After my mind left it took my physical body some time to catch up and actually leave the relationship.

In almost every relationship I was in, I got "cheated" on. It was regular for me; boys will be boys. People make mistakes, and I was forgiving, but if you keep making the same mistake, that's just a slap in the face. I had an exception with one relationship. He didn't cheat. I was confused on why he was really trying to be in a committed relationship with me lol. But even with him, I kept thinking, dreaming, and suggesting that he was cheating on me and that caused a hole in the relationship. It was all in my subconscious, it was hard to see anything different than getting cheated on. It was my norm. I caught everyone cheating red handed lol. I'm ashamed but I definitely did share of pop ups to classrooms, jobs, and houses lol, and all the results came back positive. In order for everything to make sense he had to cheat on me, and then still choose me. That's how I knew it was love, duh.

You ask me about trust, but that was out of the picture, lying was painted with every stroke. Love was a lie. Love and lie were two words were connected as one. I was brainwashed on what Love was, and I accepted it.

ATTENTION SEEKING

I never really cared about boys liking me. I knew I was cute, and I also thought it was cute when they liked me. I would laugh it off, but still be cute around them and make sure that they noticed me. That's all I really needed at the time. The proper term was attention-seeking.

When I got this attention, it gave me like a natural high, I felt special. This attention filled a void. People may say it's a horoscope issue because I'm a Leo, but I think otherwise lol. It's tied to abandonment.

Eventually I started to get into dating, and the stories begin.

It was this one dude; I didn't really like him at first. He was mean, but then he started to become consistent in trying to talk to me, so whatever I gave him a shot.

At first it was fun; we would text and talk on the phone of course very simple. Then he started walking me to class, meeting me at lunch, and all this extra stuff. I became known as "his girl" around the school (embarrassing LOL) So, you all should know my response to this, *cues heart eyes* like wow this boy is giving me so much attention. You know falling in love with the fantasy of things. It felt good.

And then it all started to switch once I began hearing the stories about how I was the "public girlfriend" and all the other low-key girlfriends he was dealing with around school. I saw the evidence with my own eyes. Always witnessing everything with my own eyes. This was just a pattern in every relationship.

Get the attention, get in the relationship, get lied to and cheated on. Woot woot!

PHYSICAL, MENTAL, AND VERBAL ABUSE

Keep me safe, Lord, from the hands of the wicked; protect me from the violent. Who devise ways to trip my feet? The arrogant have hidden a snare for me; they have spread out the chords of their net and have set traps for me along my path. I say to the Lord, "You are my God." Hear, Lord,

my cry for mercy. Sovereign Lord, my strong deliverer,
you shield my head in the day of battle. Do not grant the
wicked their desires, Lord; do not let their plans succeed.
Psalms 140: 4- 8 NIV

I remember telling my friends about my situation but also laughing while saying it because I was too EMBARASSED to believe it was happening to me. They would joke and say things like you better answer the phone before he beat you up. I didn't think it was real. It was no way that I was being abused, we were the same age...... I knew what abuse was. I saw it on tv! He wasn't some big guy beating the crap out of me, leaving me with black eyes. I was not being abused. My life was more realistic than a tv show, what they showed on tv did not match what was happening to me at the time, so I talked myself into thinking it wasn't abuse. It didn't feel like it. He loved me. The word abuse seemed to be too strong to use. He didn't see it as abuse either. HOWEVER, whether I accepted the abuse, did not accept the abuse, or handled it with grace. Abuse is abuse, call it for what it is. The reality of the situation was he put his hands on me, out of anger, or because I didn't "follow his directions" it was physical harm to a degree that I did not like. So, you tell me what you would call it?

I remember being called every name under the sun and still being told I love you within the same hour. He played mind games. He told me he wanted me and liked everything about me but mainly brought up all the things he hated about me. I didn't quite understand.

He wanted to control me so bad, and when I ignored him and did as I pleased, he became really spiteful; pushing me into walls, choking me, and squeezing my hands super tight to get me to listen to him. He said anything over the phone and through text messages to try and tear me down. While pulling me back in with a simple apology. I gave excuses to what was going on to my friends, I continuously told him not to treat me this way and stood up for myself by fighting back or pushing him off of me. But it was definitely rough to leave the situation when I was in it.

I noticed he talked to me in the same tone my father used with my mom. I figured it wasn't that serious, I could handle it. It's what people who had love for each other did when they were upset. However, I was wrong to think that I could handle any type of abuse. Verbal abuse sheds just as much blood, because it starts to affect your mental and the way that you think.

I believe the only reason I was strong enough to get out of that relationship was because I never seen my father lay hands on my mother. It let me know that something this dude was doing was wrong. Not that my father was any better than him, but I saw the comparison as a saving grace. I don't know what would have happened to me, if I stayed in that relationship any longer than I did. I'm glad I didn't have to find out the what ifs.

My conversations with myself usually went like this: "It was fine, he was upset he had the right to say and do those things, that's what people do when they are upset. They yell and release the anger, then they apologize or get over it." Most of the time the apology does not happen, and it was just a waiting game, waiting for when they were no longer angry anymore and wanted to talk again.

Surprisingly, the thing that really tore me up inside was the mental and verbal abuse. He was always comparing me to someone. Every other day he told me how he could get any girl he wanted. How they all look better than me, and then tell me he loved me. It was an emotional roller coaster for sure.

At one point I just really, really, really wanted to hear someone tell me that I was beautiful, I wanted to feel chosen by someone, anyone. I really wanted him to stop calling and texting me, and the one thing that I REALLLLLY WANTED was for me to stop answering the phone. He made me feel like crap. It was heartbreaking to even still be around.

He brought me up one day and then tore me down the next. I had friends who made me feel good and uplifted my spirits, but it was nothing that they could do because I did not feel good within. It was hard to feel beautiful because I was always being compared to the next person. So, I started to pick up the trait and do it to myself. I figured I was always lacking something, compared to the next person.

He would threaten me, threaten himself, tell me how he would beat up the next guy I ever wanted to talk to. However, he had his own set of girls on the side. I was so confused. One day we would have sex then the next day he would be cursing me out. Telling me that's why he used me and how he was on to the next girl. The crazy part about it was, he kept calling and I kept going back. I couldn't understand. I felt so low. I felt like trash. I didn't know why he had this control over me why he wanted to manipulate me so much? If he had all these other girls why talk to me, pick on me. JUST LEAVE ME ALONE. I didn't want anything to do with him, but I kept going back!

Abuse comes in all shapes and sizes. I kept saying he only put his hands on me like……. a couple of times. "He didn't hurt me, I ain't go out like no punk" "My brothers hit me harder than that." After widening my perspective when I got out of the relationship, ONE time should've been enough, but I had to forgive myself for having blurred vision. Of course, I couldn't believe that I put up with his actions. There were steps that I needed to take when leaving that relationship, but I didn't care about all that. All I wanted to do was hate him and I couldn't even do that. I hated everything about him, and everything he put me through. I hated the way he made me feel. I hated that I dated him. It was pure disgust. But I still loved him. Ugh.

I had to learn to forgive myself for making the decisions that I did. He had very abusive and aggressive tendencies. I had to thank God for setting me free. I almost had a baby with this dude, being very careless. I cried and shouted out to God, please don't let this be my baby daddy!!!! LOL. After that pregnancy scare, I dipped. I told myself I was not going back to that situation, and I was going to fight off whatever soul tie/ connection I had with him. It was not easy, but I prayed about it every day. I was praying that I wasn't pregnant and praying to God to loosen me from his control, every morning and every night. I had my friends praying with me lol, having friends that can pray with you is essential.

It was hard, because I noticed when I wasn't in this dude's presence, I felt the pain a little more, I noticed when I was not around him, I missed him so much. It hurt a lot. I noticed I couldn't laugh it off as much when I was alone versus when I was with friends. When I thought about it more, I couldn't shake off how I hurt was, as I did before. I was used and abused, going through traumatic memories, while still wanting to be back with this same individual.

I was in denial about his abusive behavior. I was in denial thinking it was just a moment. I was in denial thinking that because I hit back from time to time that it was more of a physical fight than abuse. It didn't click until much later that I understood it was a principality that I was fighting against and not the actual person (**Ephesians 6:12 NIV**). He was funny, loving, and kind but he also wanted to control my every move and tear me down every step of the way. I witnessed him struggle the battle, I witnessed what he was going through at home, and I was always on his side backing up his behavior, but I grew tired. He didn't even remember what he did or said most of the time, he apologized because he did feel bad, but it wasn't enough. I don't doubt that he loved me. It was hard for me to separate the two sides of him because I always saw the good in others. I had to break out of the relationship because it was a good sprit versus a bad spirit (**Ephesians 6:12 NIV**).

I felt stuck, trapped, and "in love" I would have never thought that I would be writing about this relationship. I wanted to forget about it all together, but it is a part of my story. I never thought I would have a conversation with this dude again. I did my healing from the situation, but the forgiveness part was the ultimate struggle. I repeatedly said, I forgive him, over and over; I kept trying to forgive, but I personally could not do it. I asked God to help me with this one, because for me, it was too much to forgive. I couldn't forget what he did. It wasn't right but I held on.

ABUSE DEFINITION

1. To treat with cruelty or violence, especially regularly or repeatedly.

2. *To speak in an insulting and offensive way to or about (someone).*

THE INSECURE RELATIONSHIP

The guy who placed all his insecurities on me, messed around but blamed me because of his unloyalty.

I entered this relationship after coming out many horrible situations, I thought everything that this guy did was excusable or perfect because he didn't hit me, nor verbally abuse me. So, my view was definitely tainted when he would do some messed up stuff. I was in the relationship feeling more grateful for him than anything and seeing beyond all of the messed-up crap that was really going on in front of my eyes.

He was a player, but it didn't really phase me because I was just happy that he was not physically harming me or calling me out of my name. So, I was easily forgiving his mistakes, due to comparisons from previous relationships. I wasn't a sucker because I still stood my ground on what I expected from him, but I did enable the behavior when I should've stopped it sooner.

I felt safe because he was nice and charming, he was a gentleman. I figured we could fix everything else, but he was continuously entertaining other females, while claiming I was the only one. So, there I was simultaneously feeling grateful and worthless, not enough. It took a lot for me to see the relationship for what it was, and look pass the feelings of security from him. He was insecure about my previous relationship and subconsciously took it out on me. It was all good. I tried, but then I didn't care anymore, at this point I washed my hands with boys. I didn't want to talk to anyone, like anyone, go on dates, nothing. I told boys from the jump if they tried to talk to me, I will play them. I told them don't take me seriously. I hated all boys, and I made that clear.

I was not taking any chances on anybody breaking my heart again. I had my guard up and it was not coming down.

USING MY HURT TO HURT OTHERS

Hurt people, Hurt (other) people.

I brought my hurt to the next person. This relationship really opened my eyes and showed me that I had issues that I needed to address and if I didn't fix them, I will hurt others intentionally or unintentionally. It was like watching all of my toxic traits flash on a big movie theatre screen. He showed me all of my flaws, just by being himself. Some of the things I was doing, is what I learned from my family's upbringing and it really wasn't acceptable to do to others. No one really corrected me, I got away with my attitude and disrespectful tendencies. His perspective was new, and I was fighting against it, because I had a "that's just how I am" mindset. Like it or leave. This relationship taught me to be more considerate and compassionate towards others, to apologize even when I didn't want to, and that I was worthy. This relationship required me to change but I was not ready nor up for it. I was in defensive mode. I didn't need anyone trying to tell me about myself, I was closed off, and as I stated before, like it or leave.

I tried to leave the relationship so many times, I noticed the damage I was doing by staying with someone new and holding on to old hurt. The feelings of loneliness and grasping onto something good when I felt undeserving is what kept me there. I felt so worthy to have a good thing. So, I would selfishly pick the relationship back up after leaving every time. TOXIC.

I knew I was NOT supposed to be in a relationship, but I didn't want to sound mean either by turning him down, I was a people pleaser. He was sweet, kind, and really good to me. This boy tried really hard with his preparations to ask me out. It was all so sweet. I felt like I deserved to be happy and get a good man. (Note: You can feel this way BUT analyze your situation allows you to be ready for this individual. I just wanted to be treated nicely after crappy relationships. I felt I wasn't ready, but I did not ponder on this question long enough and that I was easily swayed.) He was innocent and didn't deserve to add my problems on his shoulders. I kept warning him lol, but he wanted to be with me anyway. I was confused and didn't know how to accept that somebody wanted to genuinely be with me. He just knew he could fix whatever problems I had, lol. I told him about my trust issues, and how my past relationships never worked out. I told him I didn't even know if I wanted to be in a relationship. If anything, I just wanted everything to go slow. He didn't care, he could help me, HE SAID. He was ready to be in a relationship and stop playing games with me. I'm sure he was sick of my slick responses saying, "are you my man?" whenever he asked me simple questions or to go places with him. My boy tied me down LOL. I always told him I felt like he trapped me because we were good friends at first, ha-ha. But nevertheless, this is how our relationship began then ended and began again and ended and began again then ENDED. A "broken" individual with a helper.

I knew when I got with him, sex was a no go! I was more 'woke' on that level and I knew what I was bringing to the table. I was fighting off ties from previous relationships while partaking in this relationship and dealing with unknown childhood trauma every time anything sex-related occurred. Some people did not understand the spiritual part of having a sexual partner, because it is rarely talked about. But when two spirits connect it is like something that latches onto you and it feels like two become one. Your souls entangle and dance together. It requires hard work to break off a soul tie. I was not adding him into that mix.

Everything with the relationship was going well in the beginning in all areas, until I realized it was just a band-aid for my wounds. My wounds had not healed yet and I knew I needed more time. My brokenness would take over sometimes and I would bleed on him what others had bled onto me. It was a big mess. I tried to be the best person I could to him, I remember trying so hard on my end to just be calm and think before I speak. I wanted to believe him when he told me something and love him whole-heartedly, but I couldn't. I was not a whole; **I was broken with a guard up**. I could tell the lovey-dovey stage was coming to an end and my true colors of hurt were permeating from the inside out.

I couldn't trust him and I picked on him all the time. I started to become verbally aggressive and I knew it was time for me to leave and work on myself. I asked for a break and to just be friends. I didn't want to hurt him. I needed to handle my own stuff. I had been running from healing and I avoided dealing with my problems and pain head on. I got used to sweeping it all under the rug and moving on with life. I had a hard time breaking it off with him, but after one really bad argument, I decided to finally go through with it.

I had to break through my loneliness, be realistic with myself, and let him know he couldn't help. This was something I had to do on my own and he had to sit this one out. He was good to me and I didn't want to "give him up", but I couldn't drag him through the mud while I went through this messy healing phase.

BONDAGE

When I first started having relationships, I poured so much of myself into the other person only to be treated like trash. I could never understand why. The best answer I received when asking why it happened was, "I don't know, I was young." Okay cool, but not an excuse. When it wasn't going how I expected, I would say, "why stay in this relationship? Go and have fun, you're young, I'm young!" I was quick to solve our issues with a breakup. That always flew out my mouth with ease LOL. It seems like I was the only one who had the expectation of being monogamous. My boyfriends wanted to be with me and others. With my track record, it didn't make sense to be in a committed relationship anymore. I'd just be single, ya know. Everyone has their own battles.

I understood why they wanted to hold on to me while they played around, but internally I was feeling like I wasn't enough. They needed more from someone else. *Cues unworthiness level increase*

Maybe I could give less of myself to guard my feelings? I stopped caring, I stopped trusting. I didn't think highly of myself anymore. I wasn't beautiful on the inside; I felt even less beautiful on the outside. I was not confident. I was depressed. I was hurt. In my own words, I was broken.

I thought I was some curse of a person who no one could love. I decided to hold on tight to anything good that came into my life. I was so use to the bad treatment that I did not want to give up the good, because I figured I wouldn't get another good thing again. I didn't think I was deserving of anything good. I was mentally, physically, and spiritually chained to my feelings of unworthiness.

The bondage from past relationships had me thinking that I wasn't worthy of pure love. I thought I had to stay down because of the past abuse, mistrust, and heartbreak. I thought I had to stay down because I treated someone else bad. I didn't know how to forgive people for what they did to me and I didn't know how to forgive myself for what I did to others.

For You: These questions are provided to help check your heart.

How do you feel when you think of past relationships?

_____

_____

_____

How do you feel when you think of current relationships? (DO YOU FEEL YOUR PAST RELATIONSHIPS AFFECT YOUR CURRENT RELATIONSHIP?)

_____

_____

_____

Do you <u>want/ need</u> to be single?

_____

Do you want/ need/ ready to be in a relationship?

_____

Continue to ask yourself why until you get to the root of your answer.

WHY: _____

_____

_____

_____

_____

_____

TRUSTING HIM, GOD.
Songs: My Song - H.E.R. and More Than Anything –
Sunday Service Choir
Your Song(s):

Fortunately, I got better at losing my ideology of expectations of others when my relationship grew with God. However, the same expectations I held with man is what I expected from God. I placed God on the same level as everyone else. I knew without a doubt that God was going to screw up and prove to me that he was just like everyone else who couldn't commit to me. I couldn't put my trust in God, it didn't make sense to at the time. I loved God, I praised and worshipped Him fully, but I did not trust him or anyone else for that matter. My relationship with God was separated by a wall.

If I trusted God, it was the same as trusting Daddy, family members, friends, and ex-boyfriends and I just couldn't handle another disappointment. Sorry God, I can't go that route. I trust you to the extent that you will get me through the day, you will continue to provide food and shelter, but I had more faith in my parents doing that than God since I witnessed that. I had enough faith to know that God wouldn't let any harm come my way throughout the day, but as for me trusting Him to lead me, lose control of my life, and my future? That was too much. I figured I would do it all myself and when everything was done, I'll come back and say, "thank you God for something you had zero input in." Yup.

That was the true and honest me. I could not trust God because that meant I had to give him control over my life and I couldn't take that chance. I felt like I was doing pretty good with the way I was handling my life. This was the reality that my parents wanted for me and I was following society's rules. I was on track! I had earned my bachelor's degree and was continuing my education for a master's degree. If I gave God control, He might make changes to my life with a route that I did not want to take. My mindset was to not let anyone in, including God. I thought God would take the opportunity to hurt me like others did, so I didn't want to open up to Him to give Him any advantage over me. I was so hurt and closed off that I had a dysfunctional way of thinking. I automatically assumed God wanted to win something over on me or hurt me.

I made it my goal to focus on school. I felt like no one could take that from me. I viewed school as my backbone, my security, my safety net. I figured it could get me into places if I did what was asked of me, right? Honestly speaking, I was too scared to give up. I was afraid of my future crumbling right before my eyes after working so hard. I was afraid of being broke with nothing to lean back on. It was my worst nightmare. My fears took advantage of me. I didn't want to leave my future and finances in the hands of someone else. I could depend on my parents to provide for me financially because I saw how hard they worked. I didn't see God's hand in work. I had faith in my parents and I vicariously lived through them. Even their faith in God was my own through them, so I thought. I didn't own my faith in God. With God, it felt like walking into a danger zone with a blindfold on. The unknown of knowing how everything would work out. How do you do that?

I'll tell you how. I tested God and His abilities. At first, I made the mistake of thinking that I could not get into college nor afford it (**Philippians 4:13 NIV**). I was afraid to even apply to schools, so I only applied to small colleges. I set my standards really low. I don't even remember putting an application in to the college I actually attended, I just got an email saying that I was accepted. I was confident but doubt and worry always showed up before trusting God. He showed me if I trusted Him even just a little bit, He could do so much more than what I was limiting myself to. I got through college, graduated with honors, and my last 3 years were paid for. Did I see that coming? No. Did I know the "how" I would pay for college? No.

That's a testimony to just show what God did for me even when I did things my own way. When I trusted and put my faith in Him, He ALWAYS made a way! God used the one thing that I valued over everything, school, to show His glory and reveal Himself to me. After this happened, it suddenly became easier to put my trust in God, but my trust increased more and more over a period of time. I still struggled with trusting God every day because of my past. However, my healing process also created a level of increase to trust Him. Combining my healing process and trust in God, created bigger and better for my life.

SMALL STEPS TO GROWING TRUST

Trusting God was a gradual process. This level of trust doesn't happen overnight. It was hard work to lay the foundation and build this new relationship. I started off with very small things. I did not want to be disappointed again, so I took my time. It may sound funny, but this started with me asking God to remind me of little things that I knew I would forget if I didn't write them down. I was simply going to God with hope and faith saying, "God please remind me to…" and I would inject whatever it was I needed. I would say, "God I trust that you will place it back in my memory to do this thing." It was special because I learned to depend on God this way. He had become my best friend. I started out with the very minimum okay, and with these actions I lost a bit of control and gained more trust before I could spark it up a notch to the bigger things in my life.

The bigger things such as relationships, finances, jobs, and other major life decisions would come down the line once I built up my trust in God. This happened when my trust in God was a little over 50% because I definitely started at a strong 15% of trust in our relationship. I don't know what the actual size of a mustard seed is but my 15% was hanging in there.

Again he said, "What shall we say the kingdom of God is like, or what parable shall we use to describe it? It is like a mustard seed, which is the smallest of all seeds on Earth. Yet, when

planted it grows and becomes the largest of all garden plants,
with such big branches that the birds can perch in its shade."
Mark 4: 30- 32 (NIV) - The Parable of the Mustard.

What percentage is your level of trust with God?

_____

Are you satisfied with your percentage?

_____

What can you do to produce an increase of trust in God? _____

_____

Are you willing to plant a mustard seed and watch it grow? _____

_____

GOD DEALT WITH ME.
(AND TRUST)

God really had a sit down with me and told me about myself (He corrects you a lot). I was so frustrated with other people when they were being some-timing. One day they were all in and the next they were out. I wanted people to be white and black with no space for gray. I hated gray areas when it came to any kind of relationship with another person. I had to know that they were in it with me 100 percent. I needed to hear it with their words and see it in their actions. If I felt any lack of security in the relationship, I would want to bounce all the way out. Honestly, either we are together, or we aren't! I can't stand gray areas! I tried breaks and stuff like that, but it made no sense because we never knew what we wanted during the break. I liked defined roles, and everything needed a purpose. I couldn't handle the "go with the flow" style of dating for too long, lol. When I do things, I really try to give it my all, EXCEPT when it came to God, ha. It was like God handed me a mirror, I noticed everyone I dated reflected myself. I was getting mad and frustrated at my significant other for being halfway with me and it dawned on me that my relationship with God was halfway in and halfway out. A true reflection. I had no right to be mad at another person. I know if I was upset at the relationships and "situation-ships" I was in, I couldn't even touch the surface of how God was feeling towards me and my lukewarm dealings with Him. I could just recall times when I would try to fast, set prayer schedules, and read the word only to fail at my attempts. I could never finish or commit to my relationship with God.

Ex.) I participated in a fast and I was supposed to eliminate bread, meat, and desserts. I failed before the fast even started. I ate meat soon as it was offered without thinking twice. I couldn't even try to fully commit to the fast. I already decided I was going to be halfway in before I even started. I'm just like WOW. God really presented me with a mirror of my true self, and I couldn't be mad NOR judgmental at someone else who's doing the same thing that I was doing. I knew trust played a part in this and that my need to know the outcome of something before getting fully involved was also due to my lack of trust. But trust comes with faith. When you take the leap not knowing what's on the other side, you learn to trust that what God has for you is indeed for your own good.

EVERYTHING IS CONNECTED

Analyzing my lack of trust helped me recognize my lack of commitment also. I always hopped in and out of relationships and not in the sense that I was in one relationship one day and in a new one the next day. No, I was in and out of the same relationship. One day I was fully committed with the dude and ready to take over the world, but by the next week or month I was out of there.

I didn't want to be with the person anymore. I did plenty of breaking up and getting back together. Whew.

I was unsure and unstable about wanting to be in a relationship, "I don't think this is going to work out" is the text that I usually sent. I was afraid of messing up or failing the other person. I was afraid because subconsciously I feared broken promises, being hurt, and any pain. I didn't have the guts to sit through it and find out where the hurt would come from. How is this relationship going to end? I wanted to be the master of my own fate. I played hopscotch with my relationships. Literally, I was hopping in and out of breakups. Although my intentions were to spare my boyfriend's feelings, I was actually hurting him.

This game of hopscotch showed up in every relationship I was in, especially with God. I had commitment issues; I could not be trusted with anything because I would give up before even trying. I was hoping for the worse ahead of time, and I was in and out, totally untrustworthy.

I had to be honest and bold to stick to my regiment and grow in my relationship with God which in turn will help me with my commitment issues. I wanted to believe that I could stay in a relationship through thick and thin. I literally had to force myself to understand that it was not going to be roses and sunflowers every day, and I knew that, but how do you explain that to someone who only experienced hurt and pain? I couldn't take the hurt anymore. I didn't want to feel pain, but there is no way that I could dodge it. Pain is a part of life just as much as happiness is.

It is written in the word that there is a time for suffering and that suffering will happen if you are a follower of Christ. It is written that we would experience suffering in **2 Timothy 3:12 (KJV)**: *"Yea, and all that will live godly in Christ Jesus shall suffer persecution."*

You should also know that though there is pain and suffering, God brings comfort. God knew me. He knew my name, what I wanted, what I needed, what I desired. He knew my weaknesses and my strengths. He knew what would break me, shape me, and mold me. He knew what would get me to lose focus on my path. He knew my thoughts and my next move. God already knew me before I was in my mother's womb! He knew what would cause me to push to get to where I am in now, but he had to break me and loosen my desire of control and strengthen my ability to trust and commit.

FORGIVENESS

It would be a great mistake for me to keep playing the blame game with Daddy and past relationships. Everyone played their role, but I had to take responsibility for mine. I have to believe that there was purpose in my pain.

I hated what others did to me and I was passionate about the hate. It was something I held on to proudly and I kept it at the front and center of my life story letting that be the "why" behind my bitterness, lack of trust, and lack of commitment. I let this pain drive me into dysfunction. I held on to everything for so long, thinking it was okay for me to live this way. Holding on to every hurtful and painful memory vividly, until I decided to let go. I didn't want them to have that control over me. My emotions were controlled every time I thought about the situation or what each person had done to me and I would get so angry! It brought me to tears each time. I wanted to fight all over again. Fighting and arguing with them didn't fix it. It was time for me to let go AND forgive.

I want others to notice that if you do not heal your hurt it can hinder you in other areas along your life. It can affect you mentally, physically, emotionally, and spiritually. The pain I carried inside started to show on the outside. My body was literally getting sick and weighed down from all this pain I was carrying around.

Forgiveness set me free. I no longer had to carry around the burden and the baggage that followed me everywhere for so long. I learned to see the things and the individuals that hurt me differently once I let go of the hurt. I under-

stood it took time, but I took the first step by just uttering the words, I forgive
_____ (insert name(s)).

I was in chains until I went back to my previous relationships to find the purpose for my pain as Sarah Jakes Roberts once said, "go back to find what you lost." I had to go back and find what the devil took from me. I was going back to find my peace, joy, love, confidence, trust, a sound mind, and everything else the enemy tried to strip from me and replaced with lies. I walked around with no love and no trust in my heart, just BITTERNESS and ANGER with every male that crossed my path. I went back for the hope to find love, be loved, and express love.

This time I was not going back by myself, God was with me. He walked with me and I finally had the strength to reopen my wounds. I literally went back to each person I ever had a relationship with to converse and discuss all things… the good, the bad, and the ugly. God held me up as I cried about it and He wiped my tears. When I was feeling angry, sad, or happy, God was with me; I was stronger this time. I wasn't alone.

I spoke with my parents, each ex-boyfriend, friends, and even family members that I had beef with to heal and to hopefully mend whatever the devil was trying to break up and steal. On my own time, I called, texted, visited, or wrote each person depending on how far I was to them. I spoke my truth and all my feelings regarding any issues with each person. However, as I learned from my talk with Daddy, that I had to be ready to allow the other person to speak their truth as well. I gave everyone their space to respond and speak their truth. These confrontations weren't all pretty and for most of them I had to schedule a part two. Those who I wanted to keep a relationship with, were the ones that aligned with God's purpose for my life. Those relationships were able to reconcile. With others, the relationship had to end there. Although the person may be a completely new and a changed individual, I did not hold anything against them. There was just no need for relations. It was a relief. I had to release myself from my own bondage by forgiving myself and others to begin anew.

The devil was trying to take my JOY away and keep me in bondage, but I went back to find my joy. I came back on top. My smiles weren't fake. They were finally a reflection of how I felt on the inside. I did it all for me and nobody else and it felt so GOOD!

Song: Free - Kierra Sheard

Did/ Does the enemy try to steal anything from you?

_____

_____

_____ t

If something was stolen, what is stopping you from going back to get it?

Note: I am not referring to an ex-boyfriend/ girlfriend that you were delivered from but want to get back in a toxic cycle with :)

Be cautious of your triggers, level of openness/closedness, and if you are going back to speak with an individual, it is extremely important to question if it's safe. Should you write a letter instead? Ask if they are open to speak about the situation with you. Sometimes opening up wounds and healing from them can also be done alone. In some instances, the other party may have died or maybe just doesn't want to revisit the situation. You must learn to move on alone. There are various ways you can do this. Writing a letter with all of your hurt and emotions in it and then burning it may help. It is important to let everything out. It was a rollercoaster that I pushed through to ride for my healing.

Analyze your stance.
On a scale 1-10:

Rate your level of forgiveness with others? _____

Rate your ability to forgive the individual who hurt you? _____

Rate your level of forgiveness with yourself? _____

Are you satisfied with your results? Would you like to remain consistent in this rating or improve?

_____

_____

Scripture Help:

Colossians 3:13 NIV

Bear with each other and forgive one another if any of you has a grievance against someone. Forgive as the Lord forgave you.

Matthew 6:15 NIV

But if you do not forgive others their sins, your Father will not forgive your sins.

I can honestly say, once I really forgave, it released me, freed me from these relationships, and emptied me out. I desperately needed the help of God because there were some things, I didn't think I could forgive. *God please, PLEASE! help me forgive those who have hurt me because I can't. In Jesus name, Amen.* My emotions had a strong hold on me. I was prideful in holding this pain over the other person for what they had done to me to remind them daily whether it was direct or subliminal. I allowed God to be the comforter that He is to assist me with forgiveness. Praying and allowing God to take control helped become the woman I wanted to be and without a doubt closer to God.

FILL ME UP

Once I opened up to God and strengthened our relationship, I didn't feel many voids anymore. I did not feel like I was missing a father figure. I put a lot of effort to change my mindset and letting go of false expectations. It's an experience. There is nothing that I can tell you to describe my admiration or feelings towards God and his ability to fill every need.

I still desired for Daddy to call and check up on me and I still desired for my past relationships to be differently. I am verbally expressing this to explain that the desires do not just up and leave, but when the desires come along, God was there to fill the emptiness.

I wasn't as mad anymore, because I was not lacking in love. God gave me the overflow of love that I needed, and I received it. I accepted Daddy for who and how he was as a father. I finally understood the meaning of the song I heard in church, "God will be a mother to the motherless or a father to the fatherless." I thought it didn't pertain to me because I had a father. I saw him every day, but I still felt fatherless. I couldn't explain it.

My relationship with Daddy and the voids that I wanted filled by another person, were no longer the root to build on my relationships with others. I didn't long for attention anymore and I wasn't hurt when I was ignored by males. I stopped the cycle of attracting guys that did not have my best interest at heart. I no longer needed a male for security or to fill a void. No more looking for love in the wrong places.

With God, I was complete, I had a different reflection and image to look at every time I stepped in front of a mirror. I didn't expect anyone to be perfect and I didn't fall head over hills if they were charming and provided what seemed a secure space. I saw things from a clear view now that my wounds were healed. God's love did not compare to anyone else's. Not Daddy's, Ma's, a boyfriend's, nor a friend's…literally NOBODY. God's love is everlasting, no matter the circumstance it is still there and among you. Someone could have been used by God to express their love to me, and I would know yes that was God, but because they were human it didn't last long. This is why I say, nobody can compare.

I know what love is because God showed me. Love was not abuse, it was not lies, it was not cheating, it was not a threat to hold over someone's head. It was not a place to run to and from. You are love, God. Love is your son, Jesus. I could tell the difference now after going through all these relationships. I can express it better because, I am trying to reciprocate the love He has shown me.

Scripture Help:

1 Corinthians 8:3

But whoever loves God is known by God.

1 John 4:8

Whoever does not love does not know God, because God is love.

John 13:34

A new command I give you Love one another. As I have loved you, so you must love one another.

Love Me Still

June 10, 2019 1:40 pm.

Love me steal

Like when you stole a piece of my heart and never gave it back

Love me still

When I had nowhere else to go

Love me steal

When I put all of my trust and happy moments in you

Love me steal

When I couldn't be happy until I got back with you

Love me steal

When I left and came right back to you

Love me heal

Like when you showed me that you loved me more than I loved myself

Love me heal

When you took all the pieces and glued them back together

Love me still

When I'm mad, When I'm happy, When I'm hurting.

Love me still

When I tried to make things right

Love me heal

When I gave up my prideful ways

Love me heal

When you taught me how to love

Love me heal

When you taught me how to trust

Love me heal

When you taught me how to forgive

Love me heal

When you taught me to be patient and still

Love me whole.

Love me healed.

Chapter 4:
Breaking

....

My Songs:
Something Has to Break –
Kierra Sheard & Tasha Cobbs

Your Song(s):

_____

SOMETHING HAS TO BREAK

I was going through a transformation and it was tough to put this time of my life into words to explain to other people. I knew I couldn't go back though; I couldn't stop the transformation of my mindset. After learning how to heal, I couldn't be naïve and ignorant anymore. I was breaking through chains and generational curses and held myself to a higher standard now. I couldn't partake in certain activities because I had to protect the anointing I was carrying. I was going through it! I was in the middle of watching the new person that I was becoming while trying to cut off old habits. One of the two had to go and I finally chose to kick the old habits to the curve. Oh boy! The repetitive, infamous back sliding!

Throughout my journey of becoming, God continuously told me who I was, and I was struggling to believe it. In order for me to go through believing God's word over how I was feeling, SOMETHING HAD TO BREAK. This stage occurred more than once! I was always breaking something off of my life and every time I thought I was finished, something else popped up that I had to deal with. I am also sure that this will continue to happen. It's a part of growth and leveling up. You can't bring certain traits and things into new levels. However, new levels equal new devils.

In the book of Jeremiah chapter 1, verses 4-6 the Lord told Jeremiah that he appointed him to be a prophet to the nations, and Jeremiah did not see himself fit for what God was calling him to do. He responded, "I do not know how to speak, and I am too young." While going through this process I felt the same way. There was no way God was calling me to be an author, to lead worship, to start a ministry, or anything else that He was telling me. "God I am not fit for any of this." I enjoyed writing but I believed what my teachers told me; I could not write. I believed what others told me; I can't sing. Then a ministry? God how are you going to take me from the middle of the dance floor and put me in front of people to teach Your word. You sound crazy. Thanks, but no thanks!

God's response to Jeremiah created the transition that needed to happen. He told Jeremiah, "Do not say "I am young" in other words do not say what everyone is saying about you and do what I command you to do and do not be afraid for I am with you." I was afraid of what everyone would think of me. I was afraid of airing all my business out in front of others, because of the backlash I figured it might have on me or my family. Just the fear of things that I did not even see yet. I had to break pass my fears and walk in faith.

A change in my atmosphere had to happen for me to accept who God was calling me to be. I had to break everything that people spoke over my life. I pushed to fight forward to see myself as the individual God created me to be. I had to break generational curses, that was trying to hold me bound and stuck. I thought I wasn't good enough because of my past, but I had to look beyond that and understand that those situations built me up to withstand all that is yet to come.

Breaking away from generational curses and sins did not mean they went away, but I stripped them from having power over my life. The devil will always come to tempt you. However, what the devil tried to use to lure me in stopped working because there was no longer a chain there that controlled me. Though it was a long, difficult journey, I gave up the fight for my will and listened to God's will instead.

ACCEPTANCE

My Song: Journal – Casey J

I accepted everything that I had done in life, I accepted where I was currently, BUT I also had to accept where God was trying to take me. I began to recognize triggers and react accordingly, so they don't interfere with my path. I exposed others for who they were in my life. Those who were involved with enabling or pushing me toward old habits versus those who were pushing me toward my destiny. I went through the process of cutting people off. I exposed my own lifestyle and what my current. I called myself out on everything I wanted to cut out of my life. I wanted to be authentically me. I didn't want to be a liar, a manipulator, judgmental, jealous, or angry anymore. I didn't even want to use cuss words anymore! The things that I didn't want to claim were in my heart because I hid them so well. I had to accept that I was that person and break it off. I had to do something to get rid of the "ugly" that was in my heart, because what is in your heart reveals who you are at some point or another. No matter how you try to hide things behind closed doors. Not everyone saw the real me. The rude, mean, and nasty person that I really was because I had a barrier protecting me from the enemy without realizing that I was carrying some things within that were innate and was hindering my progress. When that mask began to fall off, the ugly truth side of me was coming out.

It was hard to show my true emotions to people outside of my close circle. I didn't have the confidence to express my compassion for other people, but I knew I couldn't hide who I was all the time. I had a mask on to the world. I pretended to be nice and kind, but inside I really didn't care. I showed the people who I knew loved me unconditionally the ugliness. People like Ma and my boyfriend got the bad end of the stick. I was rude and inconsiderate. Looking back at it all, I truly appreciate them for loving me through all of my flaws, through the good and the ugly. It was like once I got inside the house or my free space, I could take the mask off. I didn't want to be a different person to the world and cruel to the people closest to me. Create in me a clean heart Lord. That's my choice, to become more like you. Teach me, try me with fire and purify me. I'll change my bad habits.

THE REASON FOR THE BREAKING
Song: Refiner (feat. Chandler Moore and Steffany Gretzinger) – Maverick City Music | TRIBL Music

We are born in and of the flesh, and in the spirit, we may choose to be born when we answer to God. When attempting to walk in your spiritual journey, there is a battle between the flesh and the spirit. In Galatians 5:16-17, God tells us to walk by the Spirit, and not satisfy the desires of the flesh, because the desires of the flesh are against the Spirit and the desires of the Spirit are against the flesh, for they are supposed to be opposed of each other to keep you from doing the things you want to do. When I first began my journey, I thought to myself, "this sucks!" to be honest. I wanted to go back. I enjoyed feeding my flesh and participating in worldly desires. It was easy, doing the right thing was too much work.

The flesh is attracted to worldly desires, and as I stated before, we were all born in flesh so if you are entering your spiritual journey, you know that there will be an everlasting battle between flesh and spirit. The word defines what is of the flesh and what is of the Spirit: The acts of the flesh include- sexual immortality, impurity, debauchery, idolatry, witchcraft, hatred, discord, jealousy, fits of rage, selfish ambition, dissensions (disagreements), factions, envy, drunkenness, orgies, and the like. Those who live this way will not inherit the Kingdom of God (I was guilty of most of these actions, before taking my spiritual hike). Yet the fruit of the Spirit is defined as love, joy, peace, forbearance, kindness, goodness, faithfulness, gentleness, and self-control. Against such things there is no law. Those who belong to Christ Jesus have crucified the flesh with its passions and desires. Since we live by the Spirit let us keep in step with the Spirit and not become conceited, provoking, and green with envy.

If we stay in line with the Spirit, we are taught how to walk in the correct manner. To walk in my spiritual journey, I had to break off things of the flesh, and not look back to entertain them.

Scripture Help:
Matthew 26:41 (NIV)
Watch and pray so that you will not fall into temptation. The spirit is willing, but the flesh is weak.

WHAT HAD TO BREAK?

Throughout my life, I noticed certain patterns and issues that kept resurfacing in my life. The countless phases of low self-esteem issues, lust, procrastination, anxiety, and depression followed me in all stages. Each time the problems came stronger, until I broke the chains. I am listing out some of the things that I broke through and how I did it in hopes that you will do the same.

BREAKING LUST

Lust described as a verb is to have a very strong sexual desire for someone. This my friends came as a generational/ familiar "spirit." I was not the only one fighting this in my family, nor in the world itself. This unworldly lust of the flesh is very common. I had a strong attachment to certain individuals thinking I loved them, but it was all lust. I had a strong sexual desire for men, 24/7. I wanted them and I gave into them. This fleshly desire had a tight grip over my mind to sleep with men. I had to fight it off every single day. The way I could look at a man and sexualize him was an art. It really did not take much to fantasize and then make it a reality which is why I figured it was better for me to just be in a relationship. Otherwise I would have hopped from boy to boy, because BABY, my spirit was weak! I was not strong enough to fight off my sexual desires. I lacked in self-discipline. I kept saying I wasn't going to have sex anymore and boom, I went back. I had to get myself together and learn how to contain the lust until God delivered me from it. Finally, I chose to become celibate.

I have to admit that it became easier to be celibate in a relationship once I had a purpose behind why I was withholding from sex; It was to starve my fleshly desires and protect my mind and body. I am not saying it was easy, because it wasn't, especially if you already had sexual encounters before. Most of you know what it is like being alone with your partner in the "Netflix and chill" zone, and all of a sudden, you're not even watching the movie anymore. Let's cut out the 'fake innocence' and be on the same page. It was tough. There were times when I just wanted to throw in the towel, just do the act and get it over with.

Pursuing my celibacy almost killed me on the inside, but it didn't! I fed my spirit and starved my flesh. I was very open about being celibate, I wasn't ashamed. People laughed at me and judged me, but I didn't really care. I had purpose behind my decision, and it outweighed anything anyone had to say. To be even more transparent, what annoyed me were the people who laughed in public but asked me for help in private.

Being in a relationship and practicing celibacy prepared me for when I was no longer in the relationship and single again. I craved the feelings of sex, but I knew my boundaries and what would create the atmosphere for me to feed and feel my lustful desires. I tried my best to avoid watching sexual scenes in movies, dating, and talking to men on the phone. If I went out, I danced and had a great time, but I did not collect numbers to have conversations or anything beyond that. Sometimes I would give my phone to a friend to hold for the night. I knew what I capable of if I kept it in my possession. Doing this was a win for me. I was proud of myself for knowing my weaknesses and taking action to make them strengths.

Yet, I had to go back and find the root of why I was like this with men. It was a generational attack of lust. There are some things that we battle because of the sins of our parents, grandparents, or great grandparents. God said that he punishes the children and their children for the sin of the parents to the third and fourth generation **(Exodus 34:7 NIV).** I can say that feeding into lust geared me into making some horrible decisions. This wasn't something that I just prayed to God for and poof it was gone! Nope! It continuously tried to creep back into my life. I had to be open and honest with God but also do my part to watch how, what, and who triggered my lustful desires.

I grew up as a dancer. I loved learning routines and being physical with my dance moves. I felt the music. I used to just see it as dancing, but the more I watched myself dance, I started to notice how I began using it is a lustful act. To be completely honest I was lustfully attracted to myself. I could only imagine what it seemed like through the eyes of others. I didn't dance for the purpose of attracting men, but eventually I was getting the wrong attention. I can't really help what others think, but for the sake of my mindset, and what I was battling at the time I had to fall back.

I fell victim to lust by thinking it was something small or not lust. I always struggled with lust, but I can recognize it better now. I got stronger by starving my desire for lust with fasting and reading the word. It made me snap out of it quicker. I also fasted and cut out certain secular music to stay on track. I closed the door to my desires by breaking off contact with some individuals that I knew I could easily get into bed with, deleting phone numbers, text message threads, and pictures. I didn't even want to open the door at this point. I carried that desire over to God and resisted the devil.

Lust:

It started with a joke
Then a smile
Then a kiss
Kissing led to sex
And then sex to this
Lustful demons became a disguised bliss
Trying to ease up on me
And attack
I hated fighting them
They knew my weakness
It was generational
It was familiar
But with God I was stronger
I didn't give in
It wasn't known as celibacy anymore
It was protection.
Placing boundaries on who I let in

Flirting and having sex with men,
Creating fire to the very thing
I was trying to burn
I gave up sex as a sacrifice
To a new appetite, a new desire
My desire for God over EVERYTHING.

BREAKING FINANCIAL BONDAGE
My Song: Greater Is Coming – Jekalyn Carr

Financial bondage – letting the circumstances of my finances keep me bound from living the life God created for me.

My financial bondage played a big part in holding me back in life. This bondage almost created death in a sense. It was like flashbacks kept playing in my mind, whenever I got into a financial problem, I would remember my parents stressing over money with bills. I had the same reaction. I worried, then would get stressed out, and finally calmed down to try to figure out how I was going to pay the bills.

When I was younger, sometimes my parents would have a financial burden and they would reach out to me. I knew it hurt them to even have to ask their child for help and being so young I didn't have a job. All the money I had saved up and hid at granny's was untouchable. Any money I received for birthdays and other occasions, I saved. I saved it just for the rainy days (and gifts I really wanted). I didn't want to spend the money on frivolous things, so when it came time to help the family, I did just that. It did stress me out a little knowing that I was giving up what I worked so hard to save, but it was needed and I was happy to help my parents in any way I could.

spend their hard-earned money on my superficial wants. So, I settled for less until I got my own job. But even then, I valued and participated in saving and not overspending. The problem was I didn't have anything in mind that I was saving for, I had a fear of spending the money because I didn't think I would be able to get it back. It felt like my safety net. Though I was unaware of what to do with the money, knowing it was there if I needed it made me feel secure.

Money had me in bondage. This mindset held me back. It taught me to settle and not buy the things I really wanted; I settled because I didn't think I would ever have enough to buy what I wanted. It is a systematic cycle to keep your mindset in bondage. I always worried about when a rainy day will come and then I failed to indulge in what I desired at the moment. This is not to get mistaken with overspending or overindulging. Some may mistake this form of bondage as self-discipline because they are used to not having much. If this is the case, you continue to convince yourself that it is not worth it and that you should save your money for what you may really need. You are always thinking of what may happen if you spend or do not have the money. You are financially bonded to the fear of not having enough.

When I got to a certain age to understand the financial problems my family was having, I didn't want to ask for things as much. I would eat less so that there would be enough food in the house for everybody. I was about to get into stealing, but I didn't have the heart to do it, wellllllllllll, not big items LOL. Financial bondage literally ruined my thought process of wanting luxurious things. I became okay with bare minimum and never thought I would be free from it until I became a millionaire. Yet, the breaking of these chains had to start now. God revealed that he will always provide. I meditated on the scriptures, **Luke 12:22-26 (NIV)**: *Then Jesus said to his disciples "Therefore I tell you, do not worry about your life, what you will eat, or about your body, what you will wear. For life is more than food, and the body more than clothes. Consider the ravens: they do not sow or reap; they have no storeroom or barn, yet God feeds them. And how much more valuable you are than birds! Who of you by worrying can add a single hour to your life? Since you cannot do this very little thing, why do you worry about the rest?"*

I began to worry less and to spend money on what I wanted, but not recklessly. I desired to break the chain of living in financial bondage. I wanted nice things and I didn't want to feel bad for getting them. I wanted to worry less about where my next meal came from just like God said we should.

DEPRESSION WITH FINANCES

I don't know why I worried so much about money, but it became second nature. My parents worried about money in every way. I would hear them talk about it even as they paid the bills. Though I worried then, the real stages of my own worries began to reveal itself when I got to college. My tuition and bills were becoming a financial burden and it stressed me out immensely. I didn't know how I was going to pay for it. I stated that my financial bondage almost created death for me because it got to the point where I contemplated suicide due to this financial dilemma. Looking back, I can see how small this problem was, but as I was going through it, nothing about it was small. It was like a huge cloud over my head and I couldn't see a way out. I kept asking myself, "How am I going to keep up with this for the next 3 years?" I can't do this to my parents. I cried so much debating whether to drop out of school or not. I could barely focus on school because I was worried about how I was going to afford it. I applied to many scholarships, but I wasn't receiving any responses. I thought maybe my parents would be better off if they didn't have to worry about this extra cost. I felt like a burden and suddenly I questioned why I was even attending college. I knew my parents were struggling to stay afloat financially even though they tried to hide it from me. "Just give up just kill yourself so they won't have to struggle to put you through college." I thought about cutting myself with scissors, until I actually attempted the act. After the first time, I didn't do it again because I didn't feel the release of stress cutters say they feel. I felt attacked by the enemy and cutting just wasn't good enough, I was really going to try to succeed at committing suicide. I thought about it so much, as a freshman in college that I decided to fight against the devil and began to attend bible study every Tuesday and Wednesday. All it took was one sermon from this man who prayed over me. I will never forget how he ended the prayer saying, "You're worth it." These words helped me hold on. When I tell you, the devil was having a field day with my mind and my thoughts. Every problem seemed much bigger than what it was. I was just walking around with a dark cloud trying to survive and then amid the storm, God provided.

I got a job working on my school campus. It was my first job ever and though I was so grateful, it was not enough to cover my expenses. I remember applying for this job. It was to become a resident assistant on campus. I remember studying so hard for the interview to become an RA. I stayed up late going over questions and preparing my answers, the process was actually very long. But I was honestly praying like God this is my last shot; I'm going to give it all I got. I got the job, and I can remember my mom and I, jumping and screaming for joy. I was really praising and thanking God on another level because of how He provided for me at such a needed time. I held on to the job for 3 years, the job I prayed and put in the work for. Granted, I could have lost the job on multiple occasions, but God saved me from several encounters with His strategic plans lol. How I saw it, this job was my gift from God, whether people knew it or not. This was how my tuition and room and board got covered. I also started to receive scholarships that I didn't even have to apply for. I paid for my books with those unexpected grants. On top of this I received my financial aid refund if you know then you know! Blessings on blessings, but if I had given up when I really wanted to, I would not have reaped any of these blessings; nor witness the goodness of God. I would have been falling into the trap of the enemy if I had given up. God brought me through some tests. I had to choose to carry on even in the midst of trials. I just can't thank God enough for holding onto me and getting me to press on to see His goodness.

I did not see myself fit to even get accepted into college, my schoolwork was average and being able to afford it was something that ONLY prayer could do. WE WERE BROKE! NO FUNDS! NADA! To see my praise at the end is a bad perception because you had to know the level of desperation that I came from. God is good!

IT DIDN'T JUST STOP THERE

I knew God was real and I knew that He was watching me and protecting me. However, I was still weak, and the daily ins and outs of life were weighing on me. I WAS STRESSED, DEPRESSED AND DEPRIVED OF THE "RIGHT" GOD! This cloud of depression followed me on many other occasions, and it came back stronger every time. Although I overcame the previous episode, the fight was getting tiring. I was depressed by continuing to compare myself to others, not feeling like I was doing enough, and not living up to my potential. At this point, I had graduated, and I knew I was going through post-graduate depression. I was also experiencing a breakup which added to my state of depression. I felt like I was failing at everything. I was annoyed and aggravated at everything possible. I was living a life I didn't even want. I was ready to just break free and build a new one.

I suffered in silence, and I made the choice to continue to be silent. I did not tell anyone about what I was going through and that is what kept me trapped. I felt alone, but also didn't want to be around anyone. I was just so confused.

I Am Not Alone:

Dear God,

You said you would never leave nor forsake me. Then why am I alone?

God responded that He never left, He is always with me, for in His word it says He lives in me.

Everyone has a spirit inside of them that connects us all to God and each other. The spirit leads and guides us on this side of the Earth. I strengthened my spirit by talking to God every day, reading His word, praying, and worshipping Him **daily**. In return, I never felt alone again because I never left God, and He never left me.

I got to know God for myself and learned how to nurture our relationship.

Song: You Still Love Me – Tasha Cobbs

Scripture Help:

Psalms 139:7-8 (NIV)

Where can I go from your Spirit? Where can I flee from your presence? If I go up to the heavens, you are there; if I make my bed in depths, you are there.

John 14:16 (NIV)

And I will ask the father, and he will give you another advocate to help you and be with you forever, --- the spirit of truth.

John 14:18 (NIV)

I will not leave you as orphans; I will come to you.

BREAKING DEPRESSION

"Two are better than one; because they have a good reward for their labour. For if they fall, the one will lift up his fellow: but woe to him that is alone when he falleth, for he hath not another to help him up."
Ecclesiastes 4:9-10 (KJV)

There are times I was down deep in the valley and God had to reach very far down to lift me back up and into the light.

There were seasons in my life that were so dark that I couldn't see anyone. I did not see God, I did not see my parents, no one. I felt I was going through everything on my own.

But when I became a seeker for God, I was no longer isolated. I thank God for being my light in the darkness. I also thank God for the companions and confidants that he placed with me in different stages of my life.

These dark seasons come and go but staying in bondage and not seeking God is a choice. The battle will not be easy, but you become stronger the second you make the choice to fight back. You don't even know what's holding you down until you make the decision to get up.

Story Time

Song: Everything - Briana Babineaux

This season of my life brought me to the story of Job in the bible.

Fortunately, the bible is filled with many stories that we can relate to. The book of Job brought me a sense of relief, because although Job lost everything, it all came back to him in ten-fold because he kept his faith in God. I felt like everything was getting stripped from me in ONE season (further explained in my waiting chapter). Yet, I had hope because if God could supply it all back to Job, He could surely do it for me.

Another important theme in the book of Job that is rarely highlighted, are his three friends that came from afar to sit with him and wept with him in his time of need. I think it is important that when we are faced with turmoil, that we have friends who will put on the armor and sit through the fire with you. Friends who will sit with you even when words aren't needed, just assurance that they are there for you. To give you a different perspective when it is time to get up.

I made my own interpretation of the story of Job and how it related to me. Job was in a really dark place like many of us may have been once, twice or many other times before. God allowed Satan to take away everything that Job possessed, children included. Imagine that. When he first heard the news, Job became *naked* literally, and began to worship God. You would think that was

113

enough, but nope, an attack on Job's body caused him to be sick and afflicted him with pain. Job took this pain with pride saying, "shall we accept good from God and no trouble?" Close friends of Job came over to sit with him in his time of mourning. There was **silence** for 7 days and 7 nights due to Job's suffering. The silence is a familiar thing to do when dealing with a traumatic situation because sometimes there just aren't any right words to say (This has all happened in chapter 1 and 2 of Job).

Yet, notice that the first thing that was said in Job 3: "After this, Job opened his mouth." Job spoke, he was NOT silent anymore. Although what he said was a cursed his birth. He went on a rant letting however he felt at that moment out! We can do more damage to ourselves by staying in silence. No one on the outside of you can know what's happening on the inside of you, unless you speak about it.

Job cursed the day that he was born. He cried out, "Why has my life immediately switched from having everything to nothing, and why did I even make it out alive?" I understood Job's pain. It reminded me of the time I was travelling with a dark cloud over my head. I asked these same 'WHY' questions. God "took away" some of the most important things to me and I couldn't understand why. I began to get angry with God and turn away from him. Yet, I was still attending church, even when I didn't want to be there.

However, it was when Job changed his perspective that allowed him to get out of his rut. This change of perspective came from those friends there beside him, Eliphaz, Bildad, and Zophar who came to mourn and comfort him in his time of need. They were also those friends who didn't care to speak up when he was cursing himself. Basically, trying to speak some sense back into him.

I was always one to help the next person and be uplifting by dropping bible verses and knowledge; however, when the darkness hit me, it was hard for me to stand on those very words I told other people. In the book of Job, it was Job's friend Eliphaz who said, "Surely you have instructed many, and you have strengthened weak hands. Your words have upheld him who was stumbling, and you have strengthened the feeble knees; but now it comes upon you, and you are weary; it touches you and you are troubled."

This was exactly how I felt. Like a hypocrite. How can I tell the next person to have faith and when trouble comes upon me, I'm falling apart? Thank God for those friends who told me about myself! After yet another horrible episode of depression, I noticed that I did not ever want to be stuck in that place again! It was time for me to rebuild. I was either going forward or up, so that if I did fall backwards again it would never be as low as the spot that I was in when I was depressed. Depression was not going to win over me again. I was not claiming it anymore, and I was speaking death over it.

Prayer:

Dear heavenly father, I come before you as your child to tell you I love you. To tell you thank you. Father you are the light in the darkness. God, I declare that the thoughts, feelings, and claims of depression be rebuked from my life. Depression, I'm talking to you! Depression you are beneath me. You have no authority nor right to feel highlighted in my life. I understand the power of the tongue, and me claiming depression was me giving authority to something that is not of you God. I am claiming victory and breakthrough. I am victorious and a champion because of your power within me. I will speak life; I will live free. Not bound by depression nor anything else. I am no longer a slave. In Jesus name I pray, Amen.

I did this prayer or one similar for almost everything that I had to break.

HOW DID EVERYTHING BREAK?

First and foremost, The Spirit of God broke things that I could never break on my own.

Yet, when it came to what I had to do:

Fasting. Meditation. Worship. Prayer. Therapy. Reading AND practicing God's word in my daily life. I had to strap up for daily battles, yet also knowing that I couldn't break everything on my own was my biggest weapon. I was able to have strong men and women of God on my side praying for me as well.

Fasting: For me it is not a diet, it is not something to brag about doing. It is a weapon. It is a lifestyle. It is a tool that I used for breakthrough.

This is the technique I used to strengthen my fight against the things that looked pleasing to the eye but were not good for me.

Ex.) The *Yoplait yogurt, looks good tastes even better, but I have to ask myself if eating this Yoplait is worth the stomachache, I'm about receive in the next 30 minutes to an hour.*

Ex.) *This 6-foot-tall man, with nice muscles looking really nice, but if I go back to him is it worth me losing my peace of mind? Maybe, maybe not.*

Fasting taught me how to fight my urges.

My flesh and spirit were in a constant battle. Fasting helps to increase the fight for my spirit to win over my flesh. These battles were not something that I could just bend and break on my own. Fasting allowed God's power to intercede, reminding me that I could not do anything without God.

I went on a particular fast that was 7 days long. I had been on longer fasts before, but with this one I was WEAK. My flesh was strong. I was hungry and angry, but I didn't break. I just asked God to purify my heart. He really revealed the true desires of my heart during this fast. He also showed me my weaknesses. He showed me who I had patience with and who shortened my fuse. I asked God to push me through. I was hungry for Him, but I also noticed the many distractions while I was trying to be in the word, in prayer, or in worship. Distractions such as social media, friends, family, men, all kept knocking on my door.

Fasting brings to the surface the things that you crave the most. I thought I was fasting for me, my ability to focus, and to lose the spirit of procrastination. I had all I wanted for God to remove or improve planned out, but God took my fast in another direction. God knows our heart better than we do. He pointed out the root of why I was losing focus and why I was procrastinating. It dated back to my lack of trust and pointing out my lack of compassion for others. While I was fasting, I was very stand off-ish and in my own zone. Which was not the way God desired us to be when we fast (**Isaiah 58 6-9 NIV**).

I was lacking compassion for others, and this connected to all the other issues that I was dealing with- hate, anger, lack of patience, and procrastination. Fasting, as I learned by experience, meant I had to make a sacrifice. I had to sacrifice what my flesh desired for God. I learned the symbolic meaning through giving up my favorite foods during my fast. It was similar to turning away my personal desires (men) and idols (school), to place them beneath God.

Scripture Help:

Matthew 6:16 (NIV)

When you fast, do not look somber as the hypocrites do, for they disfigure their faces to show others they are fasting. Truly I tell you, they have received their reward in full.

Matthew 6:18 (NIV)

So that it will not be obvious to others that you are fasting, but only to your Father, who is unseen; and your Father, who sees what is done in secret, will reward you.

Isaiah 58: 6-9 (NIV)

Is not this the kind of fasting I have chosen: **to loosen the chains of injustice and untie the cords of the yoke, to set the oppressed free and break every yoke?** *Is it not to share your food with the hungry and to provide the poor wanderer with* *shelter—when you see the naked, to clothe them, and not to turn away from your own flesh and blood?* **Then your light will break forth like the dawn, and your healing will quickly appear**; *then your righteousness will go before you, and the glory of the Lord will be your rear guard. Then you will call, and* **the Lord will answer***; you will cry for help, and he will say:* **Here am I.**

MEDITATION, PRAYER, AND WORSHIP

My Song: Free Worshipper – Todd Dulaney

Meditation. Prayer. Worship. Three tools that if used together can bring out the best version of yourself. It created the warrior inside of me. I became strapped and able to fight against anything that comes my way. I strongly believe that when used repetitively they can teach you how to create a personal relationship with the Father while strengthening you mentally and spiritually.

When I get into worship, it is my time to give my praise to God while asking for his presence to come and be among me. After or during worship, I enter a silent space of meditation to hear from God. I must quiet myself and my thoughts to hear his voice. When I hear from God, it comforts me and brings me peace. I then become so overjoyed that it leads me right into time for prayer and I can speak to God.

Prayer allows me to humble myself before God, it reminds me that I must lean on Him, and that I am nothing without Him. Prayer assures me that I can break chains because God intercedes, when I approach Him in my given authority as His child. We are supposed to pray without ceasing.

I really have a high respect for worship. It is a coping mechanism that I use to calm me down when I am extremely frustrated, anxious, upset, about to make a bad decision, or when I feel uneasy about what's going on in my current situation. Sometimes this affects me with things that are worldwide issues. Worship is my expression of gratitude toward God thanking Him for everything, the good and the bad.

I was a firecracker, easy to snap and I would be even more pissed because sometimes I didn't even know why I was mad. Meditation, prayer, and worship were the three tools I discovered that would calm the fire inside of me. Chains were breaking within me. I was changing in my heart. I was changing from the inside out and I so desperately needed it. I talked to myself and declared things over my life in prayer and meditations. I was not settling. I was not procrastinating anymore. I believed in myself more and this newly found warrior was releasing all of the wonders God put in her!

Prayer Warriors:

There were people praying for me who I did not even know. It is so powerful to have someone who is even stronger and mightier than you, who has a stronger connection with God to stand in the gap and pray for you. The prayers of these individuals reached higher heights than I ever could for myself to break things off of me with just the touch of their hand I was healed and delivered. Yes one can pray for themselves but when the Spirit of God is being used by a woman or man of God it hits different.

BREAKING BEFORE BUILDING

Before this season of building happened, I wrote a poem. This poem gave me the strength to enter the season of building before it actually began. I knew where I wanted to be, but I needed a little fuel to get me there.

The poem was titled:

Little Black Girl, What Do You See?

As I stood there with a mirror stating these words in front of a bunch of strangers. I watched myself and I listened to these words flow out of my mouth and into my ears listening to my own story unfold.

Little black girl, what do you see?
I see mommy looking at me.
Little black girl, what do you see? (Holds up mirror)
I see a pretty girl looking at me.
Little black girl, what do you see?
I see a gold crown looking at me.
Little black girl, what do you see?
I see curly strands of hair; it's getting all out of place, why can't it be straight?
Little black girl, what do you see?
I see black skin.
Little black girl, what do you see?
I see tears rolling down my face.
It seems like I'm always in second place.
Little black girl, what do you see?
Silence
Little black girl, what do you see?
I see nothing, but I know I am.
Little black girl, little black girl…. Ask me what do I see?
I see a strong black girl, with curves and style.
She has great big hair and a beautiful smile.
She's different from others because God made her unique.
The world has her believe in all here insecurities,
Despite the fact that her mama raised her right.
She judges herself off of those she thinks she likes.

Little black girl what do you see?

I see depression.

Little black girl, what do you see?

I see anxiety

Little black girl, what do you see?

I see pain

Little black girl, what do you see?

I see brokenness

Little black girl, what do you see?

I see flaws

Little black girl, what do you see?

I see mistakes

Little black girl, what do you see?

Weaknesses

Little black girl, what do you see?

Bondage

Little black girl, little black girl what do you see?

Love.

What do you see?

Healing

What do you see?

Love

What do you see?

Healing.

What do you see?

Freedom.

She needed it to rebuild who she was.

What do you see?

Empowerment.

What do you see?

Confidence.

What do you see?

I see Me.

Where did you see that?

In the creator of all things, because he loved me, I can love myself.

I see beauty in the struggle, hope in the end. My God is greater than my weaknesses and insecurities. He is who was and he who is. **Philippians 4:13** *I can do all things through Christ who strengthens me.*

AFTER SO MUCH BREAKING, I WAS READY TO BUILD!

Some of you may or may not have the same struggles, or battles, and there is something else that you battle with. Proceed, to fill in the blank of what it is that you have to break.

Something Has to Break:

_____

_____

_____

_____

_____

_____

_____

Chapter **5**:
Building

. . . .

My Song: Building –Briana Babineaux

Your Song(s):

_____

Before you start building anything at all, it is important to start with a solid foundation. I had to get myself in order, become strategic with my building plan, and plant my feet on a firm foundation so I don't sink again.

I don't know if many people ever thought to themselves or prayed about hitting the lottery as much as me lol. I asked God why He couldn't just make me wealthy quick? I'm over work and school and overall tired of working so hard for everything. I had to work to build up character, to build confidence, and to break generational curses that prevented me from moving forward. Like geesh, when will it end? However, I had to understand the importance of putting in the work. I know many of these curses were already placed on the inside of me from previous generations and If I did not do the work to kill them, they can easily continue in generations to come. I decided I wanted to break the cycle. I wanted to ensure I do the work so that my success will persevere. Changing the trajectory of my family was very important to me. I had to build in all areas mentally, emotionally, financially, and spiritually because if I didn't, I would not have understood the value of what it took to break these curses off my family name and beginning a new path that the next generation could follow. These characteristics had to be put in place for when I did receive my blessings. I worked and prayed! I prayed that as I worked on bettering myself and creating this new path, that the generations after me would reap from the seeds that I have sown. I had to clean up shop and build a new foundation.

It was hard. The struggle.

TRYING TO BUILD ON A WAVERING MIND

Each time I went about my situations, my relationships, and decisions in life all wrong. I never built or rebuilt on the right foundation. I would get tips from magazines, listen to inspirational videos, and they were really good, but all the quotes would be there today, and I'd forget about them the next day. I wasn't consistent in listening and I barely believed what I was hearing so I would just use it as motivation to get myself out of a temporary funk. This did the trick and helped for a while, but I needed something of substance because it seemed like whenever I tried to rebuild myself, everything would literally come crumbling down.

In every decision I tried to make, I wasn't strong or firm. This was a daily struggle. I knew I was lacking a solid foundation. I tried to be positive, but I had nothing to help me believe in my positive thinking. On the contrary, I had countless situations where the negative thoughts made more sense, the bad outweighed the good, and everything always failed. I was used to it, so my negative thoughts overpowered everything. The Lord did not give me anything "I" desired because I was so unstable, even in my prayer life, I'd pray for one thing one week and something totally different the next. I didn't know what I really desired, but God knew. So, because of my instability, I was inconsistent in my prayers, and I didn't believe my prayers would come to pass.

Write This, Repeat This, Meditate on This, Hide This in Your Heart and Mind:

James 1:6-8 NIV

But when you ask. You must believe and not doubt, because the one who doubts is like a wave of the sea, blown and tossed by the wind. That person should not expect to receive anything from the Lord. Such a person is double-minded and unstable in all they do.

Write down your problems and speak in your authority as God's child over your problems.

Ex.) Double Minded

I speak to the double minded feelings within me, I place this in God's hands, and I command the spirit of anxiety and fear that comes with this to flee. You will not overcome me. For in your word Matthew 12:25 (NIV) you said, every kingdom divided against itself will be ruined and every city or

household divided against itself will not stand. I cannot be divided in my own thoughts, for I will be ruined.

For you:

Problems: _____

I speak to:

_____

_____

_____

_____

_____

BUILDING FROM LOW SELF-ESTEEM

Many did not know this about me in the beginning because I looked confident on the outside. I seemed confident, but within, I struggled with low self-esteem. I became obsessed with criticizing my big feet, tall height, and petite body shape in comparison to everyone else. Although it was nice to hear, it didn't matter how many people told me I was beautiful because I didn't feel beautiful. I couldn't see what others saw.

I hated everything about myself and I found everything wrong with my body. I carried myself accordingly to this perspective in mind. I was walking around with disgust and hate, and sometimes with my head down second guessing what I was wearing and how I looked in it.

My butt looked flat in certain attire and everyone reminded me of it. Lord Jesus I had a straight back, LOL. I was still trying to have confidence even while hearing these jokes every day. I heard, "You have the face, but not the body" ALL THE TIME. So, whenever I had a boyfriend, I figured they were thinking the same thing. They were just with me because of the pretty face, but I always felt like they would leave me for a girl with a big butt, nice body. My insecurities blocked me from feeling comfortable in relationships, because in my mind I knew that they were going out looking for something else. I thought that I was not enough, and it hurt even more when my boyfriends would say these things to me, "if only you had a little more butt". I would get offended, lose confidence in myself, and confidence in the relationship. At the time, it really broke me apart. I wanted honesty from my boyfriends, but I had to be real with myself first I didn't know how to receive the honesty. Unintentionally, I gave men the power to control me and my emotions. They had dominion over my happiness based on when they wanted to choose me. This crap would mess with me down to my soul. I vowed to build myself up so that a dude could never walk over me like a door mat again!

Of course, many assumed that my own jokes about my butt was me playing around. They would laugh and I would laugh, BUT it was deeper than that. I thought I needed a butt to feel beautiful. I pushed towards growing some junk in the trunk because I figured if I didn't my partner would leave me for someone else, someone "better". Even in every friend group, I was surrounded by beautiful women with big butts! LOL. I had to see booty in my face all the time, it was a comparison killer. One second, I would be fine and then I'm like got dang it! I want my butt to sit like that in my pants too!

I chose to break this comparison mindset and get a booty of my own. Everything in life is a choice, and for a while I chose to look at my physical being in a negative light. In my building stage I started to let go of hate and express love.

I never thought of how to love myself and work on me at the same time. When I figured it out, it was life changing because I thought I was unfixable lol. It might sound crazy but it's my truth. I accepted my muffin top, werewolf eyebrows, my flat butt, my long legs and my big feet. I marched on proudly with accepting all of me and started on my journey towards change.

I was weak in my mental wars dealing with my self-esteem because I was weak in my spirit. I was uplifting everyone else with positivity except for myself. I went to church, I led praise and worship, I was on the praise dance ministry, attended church every Sunday, but I was still weak in spirit. I didn't read my bible or pray on my own. I only knew the Lord's prayer, John 3:16-17, and a few other scriptures off memory from hearing other people say them. I continued to work on building my prayer life, my walk with God, and building up my spirit to believe that I was fearfully and wonderfully made. I had to be able to distinguish what God was saying and what thoughts the enemy was trying to trap me with. I started building right where I was by using Psalm 23 in all my prayers until I became stronger to use other scriptures.

Scripture Help:
Matthew 6:22 NIV

The eye is the lamp of the body. If your eyes are healthy, your whole body will be full of light. But if your eyes are unhealthy, your whole body will be full of darkness. If then the light within you is darkness, how great is that darkness!

Two meanings: 1. Your perspective reflects the health of your whole body. 2. What you watch (let in) affects the health of your whole body.

TIME TO BUILD MYSELF, INTENTIONALLY.

To be clear, this all started with God telling me how much He loved me and that I was enough. I never really read the bible, so I didn't use it as a source like I should've. But from that point forward, I began to tell myself who I was. I literally had to pour into myself every time someone called me ugly, not worthy, or out of my name because if not, I was going right back into that depression mode. I can now understand that I am not attractive to everyone and I'm fine with that now. Everyone has different preferences. As do I. I couldn't stop what others were going to say about me, but I could control my reaction to it. If you were to ever come in my room during my undergraduate years, you would see inspirational sticky notes along my mirror and in my bathroom. It was not for show, it was because I had to see those notes as a reminder that I was and am worthy! I was working hard on building myself up. It was a constant battle with my thoughts every day, but some were worse than others.

I would write and tell myself that I was beautiful. Although I didn't feel beautiful or that I was worth more than my long hair and long eyelashes, I continued to pour into myself until I didn't need the reinforcements anymore. I was fine in every sense of the word and I knew it, nobody had to tell me that.

I told myself I had more to offer than my looks. I wanted the same amount of confidence to be there when I had my eyebrows done versus when I was looking like a werewolf lol.

After reading what I wrote about myself on sticky notes, I had to say them aloud to make it easier to believe. It became easier for me to listen to meditations with positive affirmations. I became consistent and intentional about listening to positive thought meditations to change my mindset. I kept building.

While building intentionally, I realized how much I had to seek God for Him to reveal who I was. I couldn't go far in my building phase without God giving me vision and wisdom. The more I sought after His face, the more answers He gave. I had to be in the right mindset before God can reveal certain things to me. How can God tell you the big plans He has for your life if you cannot see beyond the situation you are currently in or do not feel worthy of what He has for you.

If I have told you Earthly things and you do not believe,
how will you believe if I tell you heavenly things?

John 3:12 NIV

BUILDING ON GOD'S FOUNDATION

I desperately needed this, a firm foundation.

Scripture Help:

Jude 1: 20-21 NIV

But you, dear friends, building yourselves up on your most holy faith and praying in the Holy Spirit, keep yourselves in God's love as you wait for mercy of our Lord Jesus Christ to bring you to eternal life.

Luke 6: 47-49 NIV

As for everyone who comes to me and hears my words and puts them into practice, I will show you what they are like. They are like a man building a house, who dug down deep and laid the foundation on rock. When a flood came, the torrent struck that house but could not shake it, because it was well built. But the one who hears my words and does not put them into practice is like a man who built a house on the ground without a foundation. The moment the torrent struck that house, it collapsed, and its destruction was complete.

These scriptures gave me insight to God's solid foundation. It specifically showed the difference between building with God and building without God. I didn't even have to read the scripture over and over to understand. God's word is true, and it hit me with absolute common sense. This scripture meant that I needed to stay in God's love and build my foundation on Him and His word. The attacks, problems, and situations will never cease, but this time I will not be moved, shifted, or crumble under pressure.

I let go and let God. This meant that before I made a move, I consulted with Him. I rested and waited on God for confirmation. I took a year off from work, school, and intimate relationships to focus on God and listen to what He needed me to do. I was building and taking directions from the one above who had the blueprint for my life.

IS THERE SPACE IN MY CUP? WHO'S POURING INTO ME?

Support Systems: God placed people in my life to pour into me.

Do you have space to hear or listen to what others are trying to pour into you or is your cup filled with doubts, fears, and lies?

Understand that you also need other people to pour into you and speak over your life as well. You will not always be in a season where you are strong, you will have some weak seasons. It's in those weak seasons when you will need people who are able to speak life into you the most. Having those people around is a necessity. God gives strength to the weary and increases the power of the weak, and sometimes He will do this through the voice of others.

Some of these people will be pastors, prophets, and motivational speakers, but they also come in the form of strangers and friends.

My pastors Keven and Christina Allen both spoke life into me during my season of weakness. They poured life into me by reminding me of what tells us in the great book. They did so effortlessly, and I am forever indebted to them for their words and acts of kindness. I needed them to push me, pray for me, and to continually remind me of God's promises. I did my best to make every church service to get my cup filled for the week.

I did not have many older people to look up to and pour into me, I was always the first and I always tried to set the path for others behind me. My cousin Brayon is a year older than me and we motivated each other by sharing ideas with each other.

We also taught each other everything we learned elsewhere just in case we can use the information. I also had a couple close friends who were trying to figure out life just like me. They also had huge aspirations and we all were on the same wave.

Note: Keep your eyes and ears alert so you do not fill your cup with the wrong information. Any information that comes to destroy, keep you down, or tear you down must be fought with positivity and truth. Steer away from anything outside of God's promise for your life so that He is able to give you life abundantly beyond your desires.

Scripture Help:
John 10:10 NIV

The thief comes only to steal, kill, and destroy; I have come that they may have life, and have it to full.

AM I POURING INTO MYSELF?

I took all the time that I usually placed into school or doing tasks for others and poured it all into my journey with God and self. I learned all about what Tiffany likes to do. I found out what I disliked, liked, and everything in between.

Call it whatever you want, but I went on dates with me, myself and I.

I took myself out to eat, to the park, to the skating rink and on Fridays I had my intimate dates with God. I learned to cook new dishes while talking to God, because let's face it, the Lord knew I needed His assistance in the kitchen. During this time of self-love, I also learned how to braid. I was re-inventing the new me, which was exactly who I wanted to be. I knew I could become who God called me out to be if I put my mind to it. I remember inviting God in to just be with me, I would lay down on the floor and set up two pillows one for me and one for him. I would just lay there talking and listening; I would hold my hand out to just feel his presence. It is so comforting and peaceful.

I was happy to be in this building phase because the more God told me about who I was, the less amount of bull crap I accepted from others. I knew what I wanted and I was quick to recognize the things I did not. They became two separate and clear things. I monitored my emotions and took notes of what triggered my mood and understood where it stemmed from. I was giving birth to a new me. I wasn't going to stop uplifting myself either. There was always something new to learn or unlearn.

There was something that happened to me during this time that I'd like to share with you all. It took me a whole day to complete and I just feel like sharing for others to try as well. I worked on this from the morning until nighttime. I created a photo album titled "100% ME". In this album I added pictures and videos of what made me unique. I loved capturing moments that made me smile and just happy to be alive. This album wasn't necessarily for me to look back and gaze on the past, but rather to get more in tune with myself and tune out what everyone else thought of me. I focused on what I loved and thought about myself. It was apparent in the photos and videos I saved.

November 16, 2019.

I kind of just spent the whole morning watching old videos of myself from 2016 up until now. I saved them in an album labeled "100 % ME" because it really helped me realize who I am! I started seeing patterns of all the things I enjoyed doing in the pictures and videos that I captured.

I'm a dancer
I'm a creative artist
I'm extremely organized
I'm a social butterfly
I enjoy traveling
I love old school R&B
I love dressing up

I like my face (selfies)

I love Kompa

I love meeting people

I miss people a lot

I enjoy celebrating myself and others (all the surprise birthday parties in my phone lol)

I enjoy doing acts of service

I love nice eyebrows and nail aesthetics

I love my family

I love my friends

I love ice cream

I'm adventurous

I'm spontaneous

I love God but I ignore him a lot, yikes.

BUILDING WITH MUSIC

Everyone has their different playlist of songs for different moods. I have fast turn up songs that get me hype or my list of slow songs when I'm feeling a little blue. My playlist for building is a mixture of woman empowerment. India Arie, Jhene Aiko, Ciara, Beyonce, Meg Thee Stallion, and a couple of City Girls songs to get my soul jumping. Lastly, I had my gospel singers- Jekalyn Carr, Kierra Sheard, and Tasha Cobbs type of playlist to get me in the spirit of worship. I used these playlists to lift me up and build the confidence in me that I always had. I can recall my undergrad professor, a short white lady, had me think of a song that I envisioned as my theme song(s) and tell her why. As an example she gave one of hers (I can just imagine it all over again) and this little lady burst out singing and dancing saying, "I-N-D-E-P-E-N-D-E-N-T do you know what that means?" She was singing Lil' Boosie's song "Independent" and told us how it reminded her of the independent boss that she is. Music truly does have that effect on us just by listening to the beat sometimes. Like the song Smile Jamaica by Chronixx always made me smile, and I'll be Missing You by Diddy and Faith Evans usually made me shed a couple of tears.

For you:

Your "Building" Playlist – The playlist you create when you are in an untouchable mood. Walking in your lane, building towards change and purpose in your life.

1. _____
2. _____
3. _____
4. _____
5. _____
6. _____
7. _____
8. _____
9. _____
10. _____

BUILDING NEW RELATIONSHIPS

I strived to live in my freedom, but of course my past kept sneaking up on me.

In this section I will take you through the process of how I built 'new' relationships with the 'same' individuals who hurt me. Everything in life is a choice, God gives us the free liberty to choose the life we want, but I strongly suggest getting discernment from God on who to keep close relationships with and those who need love from a distance.

Establishing new relationships with the same individuals that caused you pain, forgiveness is at the forefront. Allowing a new "you" to repair a broken relationship, you must be ready to set boundaries, so you don't fall back into the same pattern with this person(s). It takes time to discern where to draw the line so that there is no hurt for what had been done in the past. However, it is a decision that both parties must make in order for that relationship to blossom again. Just because you've done the work to change and grow, doesn't mean they have done the same.

I used the following approach for the people who I didn't want or need to cut off: My father and I needed to rebuild our relationship. I struggled with seeing him beyond who he was to me as a child because I knew he was slightly a different person now. My father started texting and calling every few weeks and he was a bit more intimate with my mother and doing things with the family which was the total opposite of what I remember growing up. I was very confused.

I was not used to this Daddy being this way at all. Honestly, I was waiting for the phase to be over. I was like, "He'll be back to normal soon." I wanted to keep the father figure image that I had for Daddy in my mind because it just made more sense.

I really cannot say that I understand my father's truth of how he perceived his role in my upbringing, but from my perspective (and my older brother's) he was not too involved with us growing up. Part of me wanted to hold that against him whenever he tried to do things with the family as we got older. It was very odd and difficult to accept. I found myself asking questions in my head like, "why now?"

I tried so hard to get Daddy to be interested in spending time with me and do things with me for so long, that now I just didn't care for it anymore. However, when he called to converse and spend time with me, I tried my best to not give him the cold shoulder. It took a lot for me to accept he had changed. In the past, Daddy would treat the family like this on and off whenever he felt like he had time for us. I noticed there was a lot of pretending going on during family gatherings, but when we got back home everything was back to normal, disconnected.

Truth be told, I was scared to open up and I treaded lightly before going forward with adapting to a new relationship with Daddy. I didn't want any abandonment triggers to catch me by surprise, gratefully they didn't. I healed from my childhood abandonment, so I didn't have a wound in my heart to feel that hurt again. When my dad left the house all day, I was fine. I just knew that he was out doing what he liked. He spent time with family when he wanted and spent time with his friends.

This new relationship with Daddy was still distant, but I was okay with distant. I set personal boundaries, for what I was allowing from Daddy and the energy I was giving him. When it came to promises, I didn't need validation nor a fairy tale father-daughter relationship anymore. Our relationship included hanging with the family, whenever I came home. I was able to tell him about life events. It was very new, and I had to get used to this new role Daddy was playing in my life.

I know I really wanted to hold on to a grudge and hold on to this old image that I had of my Daddy, the father who was never home. I didn't want to give him the opportunity to conversate, play and chill with me because I had my own idea of what that looked like when I was younger, and I felt like he missed his chance. I didn't want to fall into the trap of the enemy by thinking this way, nor did I want it to pull me away from my family. I had to learn to let go of my negative thoughts and embrace the new and improved father Daddy was trying to be.

I understood that the past can cloud my vision and judgement. The main reason I opened up for a new relationship with Daddy was the effort I saw him put forth. Throughout this new journey with Daddy, I received countless confirmations from God to let our relationship flourish. I decided to give Daddy the benefit of the doubt. As I previously spoke about, I accepted what he gave. I was able to see our new relationship outside of the old one. Once I forgave Daddy for abandoning me as a child, I was able to move forward in our relationship. I released the hurt and healed from abandonment and gave myself time to open up and form a new relationship with the same person. That looked different for me. Again, I came in with no expectations of what I wanted from Daddy to be like. I just accepted him for who he had become. This new relationship was less painful.

Chapter 6: Waiting

My Song: While I'm Waiting – Travis Greene

Your Song(s):

_____

"For the revelation awaits an appointed time; it speaks of the end and will not prove false. Though it linger, WAIT FOR IT; it will certainly come and will not delay."
Habakkuk 2:3 NIV

Patience is a learned behavior; no one gets it right away. For example, as a child you don't understand the process of waiting. Whatever you want, you want it right at that moment. It's even more tempting when you can visibly see the thing you want. When not taught to wait you may find yourself going other routes to get it done your own way. This can be viewed as ambitious, but also may result in taking the "longer route" anyway. Eventually, way down the line, after 23.67859 trillion mistakes, I learned that when you wait, the reward is always better. I had to make it my choice to wait on God and not do it my own way. Most of this chapter is about waiting for God's promise. I will discuss the process of writing this book and the process of losing control to doing things my way.

Truthfully speaking, in the simplest of terms, it hurt to write this book. The process of being pregnant with this, having to carry it, and then push it out was PAINFUL. I didn't understand why it had to be me, but I gave birth to it anyway and waited for the answers to reveal itself later. The difficulty and process I dealt with to understand and grasp the concept of waiting for God was crucial to writing my story. It really did not come naturally; I was programmed to doing things on my own time and waiting just felt wrong. It was awkward. I thought I was wasting time and failing. What I was actually doing was waiting and moving on God's time and not my own.

I was very distracted when waiting and I wanted to move, but I learned that there was more than time passing by during this "period of patience". I found that the most important thing I was doing was staying still so that I can listen to God's voice, I was in such a daily routine of listening to everything going on in your world.

Story Time

I was frustrated! I was always doing so much for others that I didn't even notice I was living my life for the people around me and not myself. I would say things like, "I went to college for my parents," but I also went because I didn't know what else to do. I needed more time to plan my life. I was stuck trying to figure out when it would be my turn to be selfish and when I would get to focus on ME. I wanted my own place. I wanted a better car. I wanted alone time and space to figure out my life's purpose, and to make sure I was not living out the dreams of others. I didn't want this alone time to come when I had a husband and/or kid(s). This would mean that I went from doing everything for my parents in mind to doing everything with and for my husband or kids. I didn't want to skip over the "just me" stage. I wanted to be able to pursue my purpose while I had no strings attached or any responsibility for anyone other than myself. I had to make a move. I will never forget how my mother told me how she had spent her 20s providing and doing for everybody else but herself. She paid bills and helped family members and friends and then had the nerve to say I should be doing the same. I thought her selflessness was sweet and cool, but Ma'am no ma'am.

I couldn't do for them if I had nothing for myself. I was not going to drive myself crazy being there for everyone else while my life was in shambles and I was in total confusion. Ma has such a big heart, but also has a hard time saying no (that was me). People continued expecting the same care and help from her years later, and she would stress herself out trying to keep up with their requests. She got stuck in a trap and I wanted no parts of that. That trap was people pleasing. Instead, I went against the grain and took the leap of faith into living my life for me! I packed up my car with most of my belongings and I headed for central Florida. My parents were not on board with me leaving nor taking a break from school, but I was headstrong about it. I had spent a lot of money in graduate school. I didn't take a break between undergrad and grad school and the transition was a lot to handle. I didn't want to rush into another "accomplishment," I wanted to take a step back to make sure what I was doing was for me.

I wanted to take a break from school to sketch out the path I wanted to take and most importantly find my purpose without hanging on to everyone else's opinions. I felt so free after I took my leap, because it felt like the first choice that I made for myself. I made the choice without letting anyone else interfere with what I wanted to do. I thought about how I was leaving my family and friends. I felt all signs of guilt and sadness, I'd miss them, but I was okay with finally choosing me. I wanted to do this, I needed to do this.

I made it to Orlando, and I was able to move into an empty room with my older brother and his family not too far from home. In a way it still felt like I was at "home." However, I had no strings attached. My plan was to relax, rest, and work on becoming my best self. I had less distractions and a clear mind. I was so happy to have my own room again to be honest; and being semi-isolated from friends, family, and other obligations that I had down South at my parent's. I didn't really think anything through, I just jumped in hopes that I would figure it out.

I worried a bit about how I was going to survive. I needed a plan for food, gas, and miscellaneous expenses. I felt appreciative that at least my place of shelter was covered. I needed a well thought out financial plan I can implement simply because I didn't want to burn a hole through my savings. But God has favor over His children, for those who seek Him! I know He always made a way! I was a witness of how He used others to bless me ALL THE TIME. I never could explain it, but He always comes through. Although I worried, I had no reason to. God covered everything, time after time. Sometimes He will use funds, a job, or a person to fulfill all my needs. My older brother, Braylan, didn't ask for rent payment. He allowed me to stay free of charge and continuously reminded me of that so that I felt comfortable. His girlfriend, Diamond, also made me feel at home by cooking and keeping me company at times. My niece and nephews showered me with love and annoyed me all at the same time lol. I baby sat them here and there to help and I even offered to pay a monthly bill, but my brother ignored me lol. I would secretly send money for groceries to his girlfriend because he did not want to take any money from me. I made dinner on Fridays and found different ways to pitch in and help. I knew how money could sometimes cause a friction between others, so I wanted to help where I could. It was a bit of a transition, but everything began to work out like it always does.

Throughout this whole process, I learned to trust God much more. I did not trust God 100 percent before I made this jump but leaving the comfortability of my home and walking into uncertainty helped me learn to trust in Him.

However, I must add, knowing that I did not trust God all the way when I left, I did my "illegal" back up plan. You know the plan that you have in case God's plan doesn't work out (which surprise! It always does). I worked towards preparing myself financially by saving before I decided to move. This is one way I devised **MY** plan.

I planned for a portion of my savings to go towards my own place and a newer car. Yet, the other portion that I continued to place money into was for my plans after I graduated with my master's degree. I desired to take a year to travel the world, to reward myself for all my accomplishments. Nice right? Right....

Nevertheless, during this time off is when I planned to write my book. I assumed this book would be more valid and worthy if I gained my master's degree first. God had already placed this book in my mind and in my heart. My view of "society's rules" made me think that I should wait for the approval of a degree to produce what God placed inside of me. Tell God your plan and He will LAUGH. I was upset because I had this whole thing planned out. I'm a planner! I'm an organizer! God just came waltzing in and changed all my plans around. This hurt. I won't even lie lol! Giving up on my plans in exchange for God's plan was not easy. It took a lot of getting used to, because He did it over and over again for me to learn to let go! He dealt with my control issues by continuously making me give Him the control.

GOD DEALT WITH ME.

(Losing Control and Waiting)

My Songs: Let Praises Rise – Todd Galberth and Bethel – Shana Wilson

I was attending Seekers Church in Boca Raton, FL and I knew I was where I needed to be because I could feel God's presence. God placed a fire in me every time I stood at the alter time and time again almost every Sunday. I'd stand there crying and surrendering. God was having His way with me. Something within me changed and I no longer headed to Orlando with the same mindset. I was no longer going to take that time to rest, but rather with the intention to produce. God had revealed my purpose to me, and I was just sitting on it, making my own plans. Shout out to Pastor Keven and Christina Allen.

I started saving even more because I was not going to work or to school in this break. I was on a mission. I let people believe whatever they wanted to. I was being judged because I had no job, lived with my brother, and was not in school. It bothered me at first, but I became okay with whatever people THOUGHT of me, because I knew who I was this time, and their opinions didn't matter. I began writing my book with NO STRINGS ATTACHED to anyone, just me and God.

TRUSTING GOD IN MY WAIT

The process of trusting God in my season of being still was fun (not really). I had to extend pass my normal level of trust. I tried to trust God, I did, but I trusted myself more. I would start doing things on my own, and then I would lean on God, then boom, I was back to doing things my own way again. It was a bad pattern to follow. It was a pattern for destruction because I would really think that my plan was better than whatever God had in store. Only when I failed would I revert back to following His way. How many times do we do things without asking God and then have lean on Him to fix it? This season of sitting still reminded me of the story in the bible with Sarah (wife) and Abraham (husband), when God promised them a son, but Sarah's old age caused her to disbelieve, so instead of waiting on God's promise to prevail she did it her own way, allowing her Egyptian slave, Hagar to bore Abraham a child when God promised Sarah a child.

Proverbs 28:26 (NIV)

Those who trust in themselves are fools, but those who walk in wisdom are kept safe.

I was always looking for a security blanket to bail me out if this book thing didn't work. That just really showed me that I wasn't trusting in God as I should. I knew part of my purpose was to write this book, but there I was still asking God for clarification and crying out to Him, "GOD SHOW ME MY PURPOSE!!!" I sounded dumb even to myself because I knew what He had already told me and I have known for a long time. He also confirmed it through multiple prophets and preachers. It's like hearing it from God himself was not enough. I knew God was sick of me but He still put up with me. Can I just trust Him?! My trust always intertwined with my financial stance. I couldn't see beyond my financial status.

I didn't trust that doing it God's way would lead me out, provide for me. I felt like it wasn't secure enough and writing a book wasn't going to bring in the money I wanted. I needed money, and I needed it now!

I put my plan over God's plan with relationships, financial decisions, my career, my future, EVERYTHING. I didn't want God to have control over any of it. Now looking back, I wish I could've saved the time and stress by just sticking to God's plan, but that's okay!

WAITING AND FINANCES

"So, what are you going to do? Did you get a job yet?" No.

"Did you start school up there?" No.

"Why did you move? How are you going to afford to live?" I don't know.

"You just wanted to go up there and get lazy." Right.

The questions and comments of others started to spiral in my head a bit. However, the comments did not take away my drive and motivation, but they rattle me a bit. How am I going to make money?

I started to lose focus because I was losing trust in God's plan for my life. God told me not to worry, yet I was on the fence about it. Anxiety kept creeping in so I would find work, but then it wouldn't work out for one reason or another until I had no choice but to trust God's plan.

The moral of this story is that I held onto anything to fulfill my needs to provide because I did not have complete trust in God. When you cannot believe fully in what God has planned for you, this simply points out your lack of trust. You have trust issues, point blank, period. We all struggle with it.

I really wanted to do things my way, the "work-a-holic" way. I could have earned money by getting a job though it would derail my schedule to work on bringing the book into fruition. I kept thinking I was okay because I knew I had money saved up. Yet, I still wanted more money coming in to prevent depleting my saved funds. But y'all in all honesty, I didn't know how to be still and wait so I signed up for so many different things to make money but being hardheaded and fast paced got me nowhere. I struggled with this on and off for months. None of them worked out, no matter how much effort I put into each job. It was basically a waste of my time and effort.

I have stories on top of stories about how I tried it my way, before trusting God's plan. This is all the way back from the beginning. Here we go!

Story Time

The first time this happened I was tried really hard to learn how to make phone cases, when everybody was really into buying them for their iPhone in order to make some money lol. I bought all the necessary tools to make the cases to get my little side hustle up and started. I had my hot glue gun, my phone cases from amazon, designs, and let me tell it, I was ready! I gave up on that quick lol, off to the next thing. I bought designs to sew onto hats and make customized head gear. That ended even quicker. I kept trying to find little ways to make money. At one point, I asked my older brother, Chris, to buy me a startup nail kit so I could learn how to do nails. It was just a hobby, I didn't really like doing it on others, so I tossed that to the side. I moved on to real estate. I bought an expensive book and paid for a class, but I couldn't commit. Then, I bought an eyebrow kit to learn how to do eyebrows. I got so good at this. I was like oh yes, I'm about to start a business doing this, but I never took off with it.

I wanted to find something I could stick to so that I could be in control of my finances. I learned how to braid, I learned about fixing credit scores, and even learned about the stock market. None of these worked out for too long because none were my passion.

The last attempt at trying to make extra income was food delivery. It was so much fun, but then I started having car problems, fun over. I was literally testing out so many things to see what my niche was, and it was exciting. This experience taught me new things about myself like my particular preferences of how to do something and how I could make money from it. It's not that I wouldn't go back to try any of these ventures again, but it was a testament to how much I deviated from the one thing God told me to do, this book. If you know what God has told you to do, be wise and focus on it and get it done. Unimaginable blessings will flow from it and essentially surpass your own expectations. I tried my best to avoid what I was supposed to be doing. There was a mixture of reasons why I failed at these plans: lack of commitment, failing to

147

trust the process, and even more importantly, asking if this was God's will or was it my own.

STAY IN YOUR LANE

God you know what? You win. Nothing lasted long, I was not in my lane. I know I am not the only one who likes to have control and manage my own outcome. I'm a hard worker when I set my mind to something because I go for it full force. I definitely went after all of these ventures full throttle. My next step would be to ask God to help me fulfill my goals…you know the ones I set up even though He gave me different instructions. I was just trying to throw God in MY plans per usual. Clearly, that is not giving God control, that's me making the plan and applying God's name as the co-author.

I couldn't ask God to bless me with something that He had no intentions for me to get into. In my waiting season, I was getting involved into many things looking for "work" and thinking about the money. I was having trouble implementing what God told me to do. **James 2:17 (NIV)** – *In the same way, faith by itself, if it is not accompanied by action, is **dead***. AKA- Faith without works is dead. I was looking for my works (action) in all the wrong places and trying to have faith that what I was going hard for would work out. I was going about it **all wrong**. I had to have faith in what God was calling me to do (this book), and then to do the work for it (writing and publishing). You can find yourself going hard for something and it will all be in vain simply because God did not place that in your hands. Stay in your lane.

WAITING AND WRITING

I wanted to put all of my focus and time on writing. I had to have faith and believe in me and God's promise for me. Yet, I also struggled with balancing tasks and because I know this about myself, it was important for me to keep that at the forefront so that I can keep focus. One thing always outweighed the other, this is really why I had to give up school. I tried writing my book after I came home from work or school and I failed miserably, ha.

I knew I had to prioritize the task God had given me and that was going to take isolation. I didn't want any distractions or obligations. I had tunnel vision. I only wanted people on board with me who would motivate me. I had family, whom I loved but they would distract me, so I had to leave them for a period of time too.

When waiting for things to come to pass, I always put an end-goal in my mind to help myself carry it through to the end. For school, I used a calendar to mark off the months so that I could see the finish line. My end-goal was graduation so I can start a career. I'm a visual learner, so it was easier for me to achieve a goal if I could see it. I had seen other people graduate from college already, so I knew what to look for. I wasn't sure what to expect or how writing a book was supposed to go. From years ago, I kept having visions about a book, but back then I didn't have a plan of what to write about, how the book was going to look, or who would want to read it. It was all revealed to me little by little, having no other choice but to wait to see the full picture.

Each piece of the puzzle was revealed to me in its right time. Sometimes it took months, other pieces took years. Completing this book was not something that I could envision like getting my diploma and my college degree. I had to wait around for everything to be revealed at the time that it was supposed to. However, if I were more in commune and in tune with God and not so in and out with our relationship, maybe I could have heard from Him faster, I don't know lol. But I do know that I was very disobedient with His will for my life and I got out of line from what He called me to do. It took me longer and more waiting due to all the expenses I incurred doing things my own way; of course, my trust issues didn't help.

Once I focused, I was writing day in and day out. Whether it was on my laptop, iPad, or my notes app on my phone, I was writing! I had no time to fall off. I had to place my focus on this one task. I cut everyone off until I got it all done.

After completing my morning routine of worship, affirmations, and meditation, I would leave the house around 11am or noon and drive to the park, a coffee shop, or even an empty parking lot to change my environment on days I didn't feel like writing. Sometimes I would write just sitting in my car. I did this for about 2-3 hours a day, Monday through Friday. Isolated and in pure peace, I'd brainstorm and go through all my feelings and emotions asking God to give me strength to release some of the things on paper that were hard for me to discuss. I asked God to give me the will to air out my own business and the instructions on how to do it so that the message would reach people attached to my story. I prayed that whoever read this book would receive healing and deliverance. I asked for strategy, but I also had to remember patience. Nothing was going to come as fast as I wanted it to, everything took time. I had to be patient with myself because this book was literally going to be about my life journey. So, there I was, finally putting my work into the right place, and it didn't even feel like work, it just felt right.

Everything worked out easier now that I was sticking to the plan, no more backing out. You have to focus and believe in yourself. Writing this book came natural for me, it was my story. It was so second nature, that I felt like I had to actually find a side hustle to feel like I was "working". I knew doubt was creeping in whenever I thought about stopping and diverging my attention elsewhere. As I wrote, sometimes the feeling of unworthiness would come to my mind and I felt like no one will want to read my book. I kept thinking it was a waste of time.

This was really my perspective and my mindset. I really had to do my part: wait, trust the process, and read the word to fill my thoughts remind myself that I can do anything through Christ who strengthens me **(Philippians 4:13 KJV)**. It was the one thing that I had to believe, that God's promise was true. I had to believe that His word would not turn void.

HOW LONG IS THIS GOING TO TAKE!

(Waiting: learn, trust and commitment)

Sorry to inform you but waiting gets BORING! Especially when you know your talents and what you could be doing! I was just sitting there pouting like, "God, do I still have to wait?!" Every time I thought I was ready, boom a temptation or a lesson comes along, and I would fail! Maybe that's just me, yeah…. this book is about me. Any who I kept getting the same lessons repeatedly with a new face on it. How was I supposed to recognize it was the same issue?

I was trying my hardest to understand the power of waiting, I knew I needed it; I was moving too fast in all things, especially in my romantic relationships. I got lonely in my waiting and I wanted and desired someone to share this space with me, but I knew that would take me off track, so I needed to resist. Go ahead and shout, TOXXXIC. Mmmmm. I was hopping into things fast and hopping out even faster. What a control freak! I wanted to control the situation if I was the one holding the remote. I wanted to decide when to enter and leave. I didn't have time to be waiting on God, He took too long.

I had to make it happen on my own. Imagine the disasters I created with this mindset. I should've been waiting on God's directions to avoid a lot of destruction and pain, but that's easier said than done.

I was impatient and I made very unstable decisions and once I put my hand in the mix of God's work, I messed up a lot of the plans He had in store for me. How did I learn to trust, wait, and commit? By intentionally practicing these three things in my relationship with God and others.

One moment I was fully committed, the next minute I was saying yeah this was fun but I'm out LOL. I was so inconsistent to the point that I could not even decide on something so simple like what movie I wanted to watch. Therefore, being in a committed relationship should have been out of the question. I knew there was something wrong with me, I just didn't know the root of the problem stemmed back to traumatic experiences. I continued doing the same routine, hopping in and out of things until Pastor Keven described the difference of heart wounds and heart sins. **Heart wounds** are your past hurt and trauma that have affected you and are stored in your subconscious. My abandonment issues, relationship fails, and sexual trauma (you'll learn about that later) are all heart wounds. **Heart sins** are your behaviors and habits that have manifested as a result of the hurt and trauma such as having pride, greed, or bitterness but in my case, it was my instability and lack of commitment. God had to open my eyes to show me that this was an issue and that me saying, "that's just who I am" was my hurt speaking. I was mad that I had to go through some things to learn a lesson, but I had to understand the power of waiting because it was not normal and not okay to be this unstable in life. I was growing behind the scenes, and my roots were getting stronger as I waited.

While everything was being prepared for me on God's end, I had to continue to be at work and ready to receive it when it falls into place. I had to believe that what God had for me already existed, I just had to wait on it. As you can see the waiting was not easy.

God needed to correct me, and although it hurt me it was also to heal me. I needed to learn patience because it took time for some things to come to pass, I couldn't rush them. In my waiting season I grew stronger in my faith to trust God, stronger in commitment and patience.

Scripture Help:
James 1:4 KJV
But let patience have her work, that ye may be perfect and entire wanting nothing.

Job 5: 17-18 NIV
Blessed is the one whom God corrects; so, do not despise the discipline of the Almighty. For he wounds, but he also binds up; He injures, but his hands also heal.

GROWING WEARY IN MY TIME OF WAITING

I felt like I shouldn't feel tired or stressed out, I was young. I listened to everyone around me saying, "You shouldn't be tired, you're too young." "Tired about what? You don't have any responsibilities. I wish I could take a break like you, but I have too many responsibilities."

It didn't make sense to most people why I needed a break from work and school, but my body, my mind, and my spirit was TIRED. They had no idea what I was carrying around.

Story Time

It was on November 6, 2019 that the verse **Isaiah 40:30 (NIV)** finally made sense. I was given this verse by a prophet on August 10, 2019. Before this date in November, I kept overlooking verse 30, and putting my focus on the scriptures around it because I felt like that verse didn't connect with me, it didn't make sense.

Isaiah chapter 40 verse 29 states, "He gives strength to the weary and **increases the power of the weak**" so I figured even though I was weak and tired, God would give me the strength to continue. Furthermore, verse 31, states "They will soar on wings like eagles; they will run and **not grow weary**, they will walk and **not be faint**."

I wanted to soar, I didn't want to feel weak or rest, I wanted God to give me strength to carry on like verse 29 said right away.

However, I was missing the middle verse that connected the two. The verse reminded me that there is a shift that needed to take place. The shift from pushing pass your weakness, to soaring like an eagle. The mandatory need to get from one verse to the next is essential. The stage of REST. Isaiah chapter 40 verse 30 says **even youths grow tired and weary, and young men stumble**

and fall. Even though I am young I still grow weary and tired. No matter how strong you are, you can still stumble and fall. That message is very clear and necessary for this workaholic society that we live in.

I was so used to being strong and pushing through to get the work done only to move on to the next thing. I kept hopping from verse 29 to 31 saying, "God, give me the strength." People talked and said I wasn't doing anything in central Florida, I should've just stayed home. I almost believed them too, but nope it really was my time to REST. I was doing my inner work to bring my body back whole and I didn't feel the need to explain that to anyone.

My body was literally growing sick and shutting down on me. You must know when it's your time to rest and take the time. You will come back better and with more strength, after a period of resting. If not, you'll burn out. The importance of resting, intentionally resting, is that it is also at that time that God can minister to you. God will reveal the next thing He has for you.

DON'T RUSH: THE IMPORTANCE OF WAITING

In full transparency, I started writing this book about something totally different two years ago. I had a different title and everything. I was looking at all my situations from the wrong perspective. When I waited, I got to see everything on a bigger scale.

To be even more honest, I was about to write this book on relationships. Fixing relationships, breaking away from relationships, forgiving others, and just transitioning in life in general.

As I started writing, I wanted the book to be done and out to the public! I wanted to heal over my past at lightning speed. Jokes on me, it didn't happen that way. God got the glory, and it happened the way He wanted.

While everything was being prepared for me on God's end, I had to continue to put in work and be ready to receive His blessings when it did fall into place. I had to believe that what God had for me already existed, I just had to wait on it. As you can see the waiting was not easy.

SACRIFICES IN MY WAITING

I can never judge anyone for their decisions and accomplishments whether big or small, because I didn't personally understand their level of sacrifice to get where they are.

I know for me; I had a high level of value for everything that I sacrificed and it really hurt me when I chose to give it up. I sacrificed my job which was my steady income that also gave me 80% off my graduate school's tuition. I had to wait another 6 months before being able to receive this tuition coverage again. I sacrificed getting my hair, nails, and eyebrows done, real tears! I had to make it happen the best way possible, at my in-home "salon." I sacrificed being able to graduate "on time" and working towards my career of becoming a family therapist. I sacrificed the time that I wanted to physically spend with my close friends and family members. I sacrificed being in a relationship, someone I could call on to share my problems with, and spend time doing foolishness together. I always said that God took these things away from me, but I had the choice to give them up or keep them. I could've gone back to school and my job, got back in my relationship, and moved back home to be with my family but I didn't. It was a sacrifice to take a break to work towards inner healing, writing, and most importantly get closer to God. I chose to sacrifice, rest, and wait on God.

SACRIFICING: PLEASING MY PARENTS OVER PLEASING GOD
(And Anxiety)

I feared telling my parents about my book because I did not know how they would respond to the news. I wanted to protect my book; it was my baby. I didn't want to hear anyone talk me out of writing it. I already went through a sticky encounter with my parents when I informed them that I was taking a break from school and going to live with my brother. That was not fun.

They had no idea what I was doing in Orlando. They were disappointed that I was not in school nor working. They had already planned for me to continue my education and get a doctorate degree. But in what? They had no idea and neither did I. So, to tell them that I was going away to write, and work on my inner healing was a foreign language to them. To tell them that I was tired and needed a break from school, did not add up to them because again, "you're too young to be tired." I was young, just get it over with, they said.

I was too unsure about my book and the big dreams I had for it; I didn't want to hear them shut it down. I leaned on others for support. I was literally fearful just thinking about my parent's response because of outcomes with previous conversations. I was anxious and fearful over a conversation that I did not even have with them yet. I was overthinking it. I was going outside of the route they planned for my life to go. I feared I wouldn't have their approval. So, Yikes! I was still being a people pleaser to my parents.

The time came when I grew confident in my work and I had a support system to keep me afloat, but I was still experiencing anxiety with telling my parents.

I did what I knew best, and I prayed that my parent's ears be attentive to what I had to say, and their hearts be opened to receiving what I was about to tell them. Even though it doesn't seem like a big feat, to me it was because it was a break in my mental anxiety and a milestone I had to reach. As I got up the courage to call them, I felt my throat trembling. I was so scared to see what their response would be. All I could think of was all the conversations we've had in the past when they yelled, gave negative comments, or found a way to make it about them. Anxiety held me back from speaking up but, I was not going to allow it to happen anymore, not that day.

I didn't want to be secretive about the book any longer, I wanted my parents to know regardless of whether they disagreed, yelled, or were all for it. I grew the balls to accept any response and not to let it interfere with my book writing journey. I knew that this was God's will for my life, so I didn't necessarily push towards making sure this would please my parents.

They time came and I did it! I finally told them I was writing a book and why. I broke a chain with my anxiety just by going through the fear instead of avoiding it. To my surprise, they were happy for me and encouraged me to stay focused. This gave me the fuel I needed to be done with anxiety and fear for good! This one encounter set the tone for how I will approach my parents with more information and just life in general.

The real-life test was, "are you going to live your life in fear of pleasing your parents? Are you going to continue trying to please others and God at the same time? Are you bold enough to do it God's way and let everyone else hop on board later?"

There are many people who have lived their life for their parents, friends, spouse, and/or children for so many years, trying not to disappoint them. While God may be pushing you towards doing more, continue to work on getting pass your fears and need to people please.

Scripture Help:

Galatians 1:10 NIV

Am I now trying to win the approval of human beings, or of God? Or am I trying to please people? If I were still trying to please people, I would not be a servant of Christ.

A LIVING SACRIFICE: SELF-SACRIFICE

Songs: Fill Me Up/ Overflow – Tasha Cobbs and Jacob's Song – Briana Babineaux

Sacrifice. The step that takes you from being a lukewarm Christian to being hot and on fire for God lol. This is usually the stage where people kind of straggle off, or don't enter fully because they are okay with being in the middle. It is when you are talking about God, sharing about him, posting a couple bible verses on social media but in the end still doing what you want to do, because God gave you free will. This is the easy way out, and trust me, I was comfortable and liked being in the middle too.

When you gave God the "okay" to use you, He reminds you with His correction and conviction, trying to push you from lukewarm to hot. I am not perfect, but I strive to be better than the person I was the day before.

True story! I couldn't even lie the same anymore, it didn't even feel right. To think I was a natural, ha! Yet, the truth just flowed out of me, creating a change in me. It is a good thing that God wants to better us, but I won't fake like the dark side isn't easier and feels good too.

I had to sacrifice my actual being, my "normal" way of living, and give it all over to God to be used by Him, WHAT?

So, like is this a trick? No. I wish, lol. I'm not trying to scare anyone away, it's just the truth. You don't desire to participate in the same things as much as you used to. The holy spirit comes in and corrects, literally the whole nine yards, changing you from the inside-out.

In my prayer I continuously asked God to increase in my life and to decrease me. I needed more of Him and less of me.

BIG SACRIFICES FOR BIG RESULTS

The size of your blessings depends on the size of your sacrifice. I broke a lot of chains on the inside of me to get to where I am right now, and I don't plan on going backwards. God provided the fire, and I provided the sacrifice. The sacrifice grew bigger and bigger each time. My two biggest investments were my money and my sleep. I had to pour into this book (the entire journey) financially, but also, miss out on a lot of sleep.

Whatever I sacrificed usually came back to me in more ways than I expected. I persisted until I reached my goal. I was trying to make the best of the situation. God literally knew what I needed, and it helped me not to settle. Whatever and whoever, I had to sacrifice, and I did it unapologetically.

I was desperate for change, I was crying, kicking, and screaming to God for change. I wanted different results than before. The mental, physical, financial and every other cycle was stopping here, I was not going backwards no matter what.

What are your <u>top three values</u> that you would sacrifice for GREAT change? The size of your sacrifice matters.

Ex.) Abraham is going to sacrifice his own offspring, Isaac. I'm not saying go throw your child into the fire pit, please no; but to understand context of Abraham's big sacrifice to his great fortune (Genesis 22).

_____

_____

_____

_____

What habits are inhibiting you from pursuing God's plan for you?

Ex.) Thinking about the judgment from others _____

_____

_____

_____

SACRIFICES AND FINANCES

Story Time

I had finally made the decision to give a huge tithe to my church. It took me 18 days to give myself the pep talk and talk myself into doing it because money was scarce at the time. It was a battle to fight the double minded thoughts in my head. It wasn't even like it was a real sacrifice anyway because I was giving back to God what He lent to me. That's how much of a hold the devil had on me. That chain of financial bondage had really been there for generations. It was deeply invested, but I knew I had to break this chain. With this money I had to think and act like I had already given it away. I told myself where it was going when I took it out of the bank, I subtracted it from my budget, and well it's gone. This was not very easy for me because the enemy was after my mind to make me stay in belief that I couldn't make it another day without saving this money and using it for myself instead.

I strapped up and prepared for war when the games of being double minded tried to take stabs at me. I had to pour the word of God over my own thoughts and decisions because my words could fail, my words could come back void, however, God's word could not. I prayed over the money, asked God to break financial chains from my family, and for the many generations after. I planted my seed and felt a release after doing so. I felt so much joy, I was intentional about depositing the money and I knew God was proud. I didn't tell anybody about it, I was very focused about just getting to church to plant my seed that day. I felt an increase in faith and trust before I got to church, and I felt even better after I left. The job was D-O-N-E. I had the faith to plant a $1,000 seed and I literally received the money back within a week. God works in mysterious ways.

Scripture Help:

2 Corinthians 9: 6-8 NIV

Remember this: Whoever sows sparingly will also reap sparingly, and whoever sows generously will also reap generously. Each of you should give what you have decided in your heart to give, not reluctantly or under compulsion, for God loves a cheerful giver. And God is able to bless you abundantly, so that in all things at all times, having all that you need, you will abound in every good work.

SACRIFICING AND COPING WITHOUT GOD

First let's talk about what a coping mechanism is. Coping mechanisms are your strategies that you automatically implement when placed in stressful or traumatic situations.

Everyone has their personal coping methods to deal with unwanted situations. Some shut down, scream, run or fight, and anything else that will get them out of the situation quick. I had to sacrifice some of my favorite coping mechanisms, because it's what I ran to at the sight of trouble instead of running to God. So, hint, hint my number 1 go to, was running away from my situations. I ran away from my problems all the time. Even if it meant running to my bed to sleep so I can avoid thinking about the problem.

I did it as a child and as an adult. As a kid I ran to the bathroom and locked the door. I did this especially whenever I knew I was about to get in trouble. It worked most of the time because I would stay in the bathroom for hours. Because that was my go-to spot, I used to pack snacks in there and everything. I know, nasty, right? I even had my portable game in there with me, camping out. I was serious. By the time I snuck out, my parents would sometimes forget why they were even upset. It only enabled me to believe that running away would solve my problems, because my parents would rarely punish me after I got out of the bathroom.

However, later down the years this same coping mechanism stuck with me. Innocently, I even thought about going to college as running away. It was always my plan to leave my house, I wanted out lol. I also wanted my own space. I ran from all the trouble I had a home. I didn't want to be too far, but far enough that I can do as I pleased without anyone bothering me, so I figured 3-5 hours away was perfect. Luckily, for me I attended a school 30 minutes away.

The problem with running away was that whenever I came back, the issue was still there. It will always set me off and triggered me in such a way that I was mentally broken. After graduating college, I went right back to that place, the same place where the same problem still lingered even after years. As soon as I stepped foot in the door, I tried to run away. I wanted to get an apartment right after I graduated from college, but there was no way that God was letting that happen. He was letting me face my problems head on, no more running away. This is when I started to work through my abandonment issues with my father. I was participating in equine therapy and really healing my wounds. What I learned from equine therapy was that I had to face my fear and not run away from them. However, I still wanted to move so that I can live on my own now that I was a graduate. I did move to Orlando, and I wanted to ensure that it wasn't just another running away episode. I knew that instead, I needed to run to God for healing. Too bad I had yet another lesson to learn.

COPING WITH ALCOHOL

In my junior year in college, I learned yet another coping mechanism! Woooo, alcohol.

I didn't start drinking to look or feel cool. People tried to get me to drink alcohol all the time, it didn't work until it was something I wanted to do on my own. I started drinking, due to curiosity. I wanted to know how it made me feel and whether it would take all my problems away. I had never been drunk before. Let's try it. Boom, it made everything worse (for me) especially the day after, feeling guilty and ashamed but during, it took my mind off all of my anxiety and problems.

I used alcohol as a coping mechanism to run from certain problems I was dealing with at the time. Sure, it erased the hurt temporarily, but it was good enough for now. Eventually I knew I had to make the choice to stop drinking to get so drunk and become someone who actually dealt with her problems. It was deeper than just drinking. I was drinking with purpose.

Liquor helped me run away. I was doing it to become someone else or just straight black out, and not be anyone. For others it may be drugs, or maybe not even a substance. Sometimes people dive into their work so much and stay busy so that they don't have to deal with what they have at home. Alcohol, job, drugs, whatever your vice is, it is a ploy to get out of your responsibilities, out of dealing with what's really bothering you. This never solved the problem, you just prolong fixing it and in essence, added more problems in the midst. The problem met you right back in your face when you were back home/ sober. Yay. Lesson learned, face your problems.

SACRIFICE AND SURRENDERING
My Song: Withholding Nothing – William McDowell

As I waited while you made a way on my behalf God, I had to surrender and sacrifice everything that I was putting over you. You knew where I would fall weak, but your grace was sufficient for me. You used your strength in my weakness to build me stronger as I waited. I chased the thoughts of marriage. I chased money, I chased everything else but you.

I would give it all up over and over again. I continue to surrender and fall on my face especially when I get too far ahead of myself thinking I can do anything without you.

I freely give myself away to you God.

Scripture Help:
2 Corinthians 12:9 NIV

But he said to me, "My grace is sufficient for you, for my power is made perfect in weakness." Therefore, I will boast all the more gladly about my weaknesses, so that Christ's power may rest on me.

Chapter 7 :
Stop Faking The Funk

· ·

My Song: God is Here – Karen Clark-Sheard

Those who are kind benefit themselves, but
the cruel bring ruin on themselves.
Proverbs 11:17 NIV

I was tired of pretending to be perfect. I was tired of pretending to be normal. I was tired of selling myself short because other people weren't on my level of thinking and dreaming.

My anger, depressive episodes, and personal issues started to slip out in front of others, and then spill over onto them. I didn't like what it was doing to me or who I was becoming by withholding so much pain. I wanted to get help. I didn't want to pretend like I was not hurting to look good in front of people. This is where I couldn't "fake the funk" anymore.

How could I be on a journey to be a therapist, wanting help others heal, but feel every trigger that my clients are going through within myself? How could I push so hard for therapy, while not valuing therapy for myself?

I needed the alter calls, I needed prayers, and I needed therapy in order to learn how to heal from all of my wounds.

I stopped running to everyone else and ran to the only one who could touch me and heal my heart, God.

I finally went to lay my burdens down at the altar, stretched out on the floor laying in tears I turned them over to God. That was the most important step in the process of how I let it all go.

IT'S A PROCESS

In the past mental health was often overlooked and had a negative connotation overall. Especially in the black community. If therapy was offered, people would think, "she's crazy." Professionally it could be an underpaying career to get into.

Everything is connected to your mental stability because it is your mindset that helps you fail or succeed, allow you to remain positive or negative when you enter any situation, subject, or field. Mental illness does not have a specific target on whom it attacks, so it is found everywhere and in anyone. Mental illness can be connected to other diagnosis in other fields. Someone may become depressed due to battling serious health issues, such as cancer or lupus. When people go through issues, they deal with more than just one thing. Many times, it is a rippling effect and many areas in one's life can be affected all at once.

Fortunately, mental health has now become the main topic and finally receiving the attention it deserves due to individuals with influence speaking up publicly. Influencers and public figures brought awareness to their communities and surrounding areas.

I always wanted to go into counseling/therapy, but I noticed I overlooked how important mental health was because of my lack of knowledge. I experienced issues, but never thought mental illness applied to me. Getting information about depression, anxiety, and attention deficit/hyperactivity disorder (ADHD) was not a thing in my black household growing up. I overlooked my own mental issues because I thought they were small and didn't matter. It was not something that I could see, I couldn't put a name on it or label what was going on with me therefore, I ignored it. I was also unaware of the hurt and pain that I was going through because I normalized my pain; ignorance can definitely be bliss.

In **Hosea 4:6,** God said His people are killing themselves because of lack of knowledge. I caused myself more hurt and pain from ignoring what I was going through, but the more knowledge and awareness I came across, the more comfortable I became in accepting my issues. Knowing how to recognize my problems and get help made me less stressed and more accepting of what I was going through.

The more people prolong the process by ignorance, that more hurt and pain they'll cause to themselves. Many times, people know they have a problem but are scared to address it. Although it may be invisible to others, it is more valuable for you to go through the process of unraveling the hurt that others can't see and stick with the process no matter how long, or how crazy you look to other people. I was fighting battles privately that only God and I knew about.

Some don't understand that if you aren't connected to the vine, the devil can take control of your mind. That's how he wins you, in your mind by selling you the fast dreams, the quick schemes. But with God you dream bigger! You achieve bigger! However, it's a harder fight because it's a responsibility, a commitment. It's easier and quicker to get what the devil has for you. I know I personally didn't want to wait for what God had for me. I wanted fast results, but that's why it's easier for the enemy to grasp your attention. With God he takes his time with you for long lasting results. He's pushing you to build the characteristics in you.

YEAH, YOU'RE PRETTY BROKEN
Song: Get It Together - India Arie

The main part that I like about this song is when she says: "16 years are showing up on your face and you only have yourself to blame if you continue to live this way."

You've been dealing with the same issues for years and it's showing on your face.

I stopped faking the funk and got very real with myself cause the truth was, I HAVE ISSUES! Issues that were not too big or too small for God and I desired to get them fixed!

I was ready for therapy! I got serious about it this time because before in the past when I attempted to attend therapy, I used to skip over some of the questions when filling out forms. This time I made an agreement with myself to be vulnerable, open, and honest about everything. I was ready for healing and I could not get it if I was not going to be honest and intentional about my issues.

I didn't want to make excuses anymore, I didn't have to say, "ehhh you don't really have that issue, it's all in your head Tiffany." Nope, I wanted to write it all down so it can be discussed later in my sessions. If it were any type of issue that had been bothering me for years, I wanted to talk about it! I went in there with the motive to work on abandonment, my self-esteem, lack of trust and aggression. I lied to myself too many times and opted out telling myself that I don't need to go to therapy to talk about it. They all needed to be addressed at some point and I was not there to click the "save for later" option any longer. It was time to release.

I was excited for therapy to be my space to freely talk and express all of my concerns without judgement. I requested to express my emotions before my therapist even began to speak. I wanted to ensure that there was no bias and everything I stated were my own thoughts and emotions. He was focused on what I was expressing.

There are times when no one may understand your pain and why you are feeling the way that you are; however, deal with the emotions that come to the surface and spend some time alone to reflect before talking to the next person about it. No one will be able to feel exactly how you do at the moment. Some could compare if it happened to them and it would be nice to get that feedback and share, but after you have understood your own feelings.

CONFESSIONS OF MY PAIN
My Song: Confessions - Usher
"If I'm gonna tell it, then I gotta tell it all!"

In order to heal you have to know where you are broken. This was definitely the chapter I struggled writing about, but I am no longer silent.

So, here I was trying therapy again for the fourth time. This time I was intentional, this time I broke a chain. Towards the end of my first therapy session, my therapist asked me if there was anything that I had never said to anyone before. I remember the tears welling up in my eyes before I uttered the word "molested" for the first time. Immediately tears ran down my face.

I went back to the many nights I stayed up crying about being molested. I remember crying myself to sleep when I was younger. Sometimes I would run to my mom's room and get in bed with her, she was my comforting place. I didn't want to deal with it, but I couldn't tell her what happened to me either. I was too scared. I just wanted the pain to go away, I wanted God to take the thoughts away, I just couldn't bear it. I couldn't bear the pain, it hurt me so much I pushed it deep down inside of me in a place I couldn't see it anymore. I suppressed the thoughts. The emotions would pop up again from time to time, throughout the years and I would push them back down again. I kept myself busy, so I didn't have time to figure out why I was hurting anymore. I became numb.

However, as I got older these emotions started to stir up in me more frequently. Every time I heard about sexual trauma or saw it, I was triggered. I was afraid to open up those emotions because it meant that I really had to deal with this hurt. At this point I didn't even understand why I was crying anymore, because as I said I kind of forced myself to forget about what happened to me as a child. As usual, I told myself that it wasn't a big deal when things happened to me. I kept shutting it out of my mind. I remember repetitively saying, "this didn't happen to me, you don't need to cry about it, it's not that serious." I would say and do anything to get the thought out of my head. I didn't want to speak up about it bothering me. I wanted to keep peace amongst myself and everyone else. I didn't want to relive the hurt. I couldn't tell anyone. Even when I tried to pace myself to talk about it before, NOTHING CAME OUT. Before I could speak, I wrote. Allowing myself to write it out so that I could put it into words for others to understand helped me.

EMBRACING MY HEALING

During this time, I was getting stronger in my spiritual journey. I was meditating more, focusing on who I was becoming as an individual, and building a relationship with God. I was not as involved in too many things, like I was in high school and college, I wasn't in a relationship; it was literally just God and me. In the midst of it all, it was God and I slaying demons fighting my internal battles. I invested more time in my relationship with God. Slowly, I began to hear His voice more and follow His lead. In my time of worship and meditation with God, is when He stirred up in my thoughts, what felt like an instant replay of me being molested.

Before I came to my place of peace and healing, I used to see it as God trying to hurt me, like every other male I was hurt by before. Other times I used to rebuke it because I thought it was the devil trying to attack me. I had a defensive mindset and chose to run away when these thoughts came to me. Yet, through it all, I thank God for waiting for me, for being patient with me as I succumb to His power. I had to accept his power and change my mindset from defensive to embracing His healing powers.

When your body is at peace or quiet enough to listen, the Holy Spirit will lead you to certain memories to get you to heal in those areas. For me it was to heal about being molested at such a young age, for you it may be something else. I'm sharing this because I didn't know that God wanted me to isolate so that I can deal with this. It seems as though He brings up the memories to hurt you, but it is not to cause disruption in your life but to fix, heal, and bring the pieces of your heart to a whole. Sometimes we don't even know why we act or why we feel certain ways especially when it comes to certain people, but in time it will be revealed. If you keep an open mind, the Spirit will reveal it to you in due time. Only if you are intentional about allowing the Healer in. You must be intentional about going through the valley to find the roots of your problems. Again, I will quote this scripture, *"For He wounds, but he also binds up; He injures, but his hands also heal" Job 5:18.* God is my healer.

I was in disbelief for such a long time, but the incident kept replaying itself in my head, and I was silently crying myself to sleep at night all over again! The mind is a tricky place. This issue had been bothering me since I was a child. I waited until I was in my 20's to decide it was time to talk about it. To feel the emotions that were released once I said it out loud to someone else was something that I could not fake. The tears rolled down my face and I literally could not speak after I said the word "molested". My mind went everywhere but my mouth was mute. I held it in for so long that it had a tight grip on me. I could not speak, I could not think, I had not even told this to my parents nor my closest friends. No one knew this about me, and I finally said it. I didn't believe it was real. I thought it shouldn't hurt that much because it was just molestation and not rape. Boy was I wrong! Only thing I knew to do was to be grateful that what happened to me was not much worse. I never dealt with the problem because I was taught to be grateful that whatever I go through is not worse than what it could be. However, that mindset, without acknowledging my pain set me up for failure. It shut me out of my own emotions. You are allowed to feel how you feel. Being molested revealed itself to be a big problem that I shoved into a small bottle.

I had to deal with this issue for what it really was. I had to be real with myself and let it out because I held on to that hurt for so long that it handicapped me from becoming all God wanted me to be. I thought I was a strong person because I held on to a secret, but once I released it out loud, I realized how much stronger I was by being open and vulnerable.

This incident occurred at the tender age of 8. At such a young age I was exposed to being used by a male figure. I didn't know exactly what was going on at the time, but I knew it was wrong and how I FELT. As an adult, I struggled when having any sexual encounter with males. I giggled and squirmed because it reminded me of the time I was touched involuntarily. I felt like I was being used even though I was consenting to having sex. To avoid those feelings, I would start arguments if I didn't get attention, cuddles, or confirmation with words that they still wanted me after the love making was over. I would yell accusing my boyfriend of using me or I would silently cry, become passive aggressive. It was a trigger; I didn't even want to participate in sex because I couldn't enjoy anything.

Whenever I saw this touchy subject in a movie or heard someone talk about sexual abuse, my spirit would begin to weep because I too was hurting and needed to be healed in those areas. I was instantly saddened that not only it happened to the person, but that I could relate to that person's story. I would often think and feel the emotions for others and wondered if other young girls have gone through the same. It was a constant thought in my mind.

Moreover, I carried other trauma with me. Not only did I have the issue of molestation, but I also still dealt with the feeling of abandonment which led to the mistreatment and abuse in my relationships. At some point, I went through my extended phase of not wanting to be in a relationship ever again, and men ain't **bleep**. However, I didn't want to live in my bitterness forever.

I was able to release and get out of the bondage of feeling like I had to keep my issues to myself and it helped tremendously. It became easier for me to cope with all my issues because I was more open to talking about them in front of others now. I could openly talk about my trash treatment with my exes to my friends. But when it came to molestation and being abused, I felt so guilty and ashamed. I never wanted to bring it up. Personally, when being molested, I blamed myself for the whole thing because I knew my mother taught me better than that. Although my mom told me to let her know if anyone ever touched me in my "private areas", I thought because I knew this person it was okay. They weren't a stranger to me.

Then as I got older, I felt even more ashamed for being naive because at the time I did not think it was "bad" because I enjoyed the attention, and it was a very playful encounter. I remember smiling and laughing with this person because we were playing before the situation occurred. So, I felt safe when he touched me inappropriately. I felt secure, I knew him. I thought it was safe and fun because of our environment even though I didn't like the act itself. However, I liked the consistent attention. I knew it was wrong though. I didn't have a good feeling about it, and he always told me to "shhh", so I kept it to myself. Once I got older and found out the true definition of molestation, I realized how bad it really was. I was angry at the inner child in me for getting molested, "are you stupid? How could you let someone do that to you? And then you kept going back!" I definitely withheld the information from everyone that I knew. I didn't want to be labeled dumb and naïve. I let the shame and guilt take over, creating a huge wall that pushed me from letting people get close to me.

I didn't want to accept that I was only 8 years old when it occurred and that I was scared to speak up. There were giggles and laughs while it was occurring, I thought this person loved me. He used my body, he played with me in secrecy and under the covers and I couldn't get over feeling used. I remember even seeing him with another girl, but I was so starry-eyed for him that it didn't make a difference. I still wanted the attention. I wanted this dude to choose me over the older girl he was trying to talk to down the street, lol. So, if that meant letting him touch me under the covers, I did it. As a child you can be very vulnerable and innocent to this world, lacking knowledge and attaching to anyone and anything.

I just knew my mom would be furious with me if I ever told her, because she warned me not to do those things. The feelings of guilt and shame continued to linger with me and kept me silent. However, by the end of therapy I was openly speaking about being molested and sharing more insight about the story. I had to unravel the years of hurt to get to where I am now. If I didn't, I would still be caught up in the web. There were big problems I released in therapy, that I shoveled into a small bottle throughout the years. I didn't speak on my feelings because I wanted to protect others and myself from any backlash. I had to forgive myself because a lot of things I went through, weren't my fault. I put so much blame on myself.

It was hard to separate the feelings of happiness and excitement and giggles from the sexual trauma because that's what it started off as. I had to continually tell myself, "it's okay to put the blame on someone else, you were a child. Think of how you feel about molestation now, you wouldn't want that for your nieces or nephews even if they told you they enjoyed it." I enjoyed the giggles before, but when he started to touch me inappropriately, I didn't enjoy that part. Then the pain and suffering that came along with feeling used after the molestation was painful especially as a child. To think that he didn't really want me, that damaged me even more.

I was extremely mad at my younger self for being so stupid and letting someone touch me. It wasn't right. How could I let this happen? I was smart, and that was such a stupid decision. I just realize how easy it is to let more situations like this occur due to childhood trauma. I wanted the attention from men, I wanted to be loved, held, and comforted. I didn't know how to tell it to my father, so I reached out to others.

In chapter 2, I touched on the subject of my unknown childhood trauma and how it related to my relationships, and when anything sex-related occurred, this trauma would simply come to the surface and openly display emotions I felt deeply within.

In each relationship I noticed how I wanted to make sure the person liked me or chose me before I could securely commit. I longed for protection and attention. I wanted my man to give me everything I lacked. I learned the hard way that I couldn't put that pressure and trust in a man to fulfill that. I learned that my happiness was solely my responsibility and no one else's.

I would easily jump in and out of a relationship if I felt unsecured or unstable. I would break up with the person and get back with them making it a toxic cycle without realizing I was also providing a lack of security for the other person. I didn't know how to not feel used and I wanted to protect myself. Therapy helped me figure out the stem to the problem, interrupted my cycle of thoughts and patterns, and I was able to identify my triggers much easier.

Abandonment + Sexual Trauma + Low Self-Esteem = Latching onto Anyone Who Provided Security

SEXUAL ABUSE AND SEXUAL ASSAULT NORMALCY

Sexual abuse and assaults had been my normal for so long, that it was something I didn't even want or care to speak up about when it happened. As a child, I witnessed and dealt with boys smacking my butt, grabbing on tits and my vagina just as a normal encounter when passing them by in the hallway. It was not new to me. Males being groped and raped by women and never speaking up about it was uncommon, but it all happens so I again, I thought it was normal. I believe that speaking up on these occurrences directly and indirectly can create a shift to highlight and bring to the surface that this is not okay. If you have committed the act, confess, apologize, and **turn away** from your wicked ways. An apology may not be sufficient for the victim, but you aren't doing any justice by continuing the act. Forgiveness plays a huge role for both parties involved, at the right time. Personally, it was the only thing that set me free. Individuals are speaking up about these encounters left and right. It is no longer being brushed off as easily.

With this same topic, it is not, nor will it ever be okay to make false accusations. Needless to say, live in your truth.

I do believe that normalizations helped me ignore and brush off my encounters of being touched inappropriately. Besides the matter if I fussed someone out or hit back, in society it was acceptable and unspoken about, easy for people to get away with it. However, things are changing now.

Stop Faking the Funk Activity
Reclaiming MY feelings and releasing them:
Below I wrote out all my emotions that I felt towards this not so "big deal" incident to find out that it was very much a big deal to me and affected my life.

You are hurt Tiffany. Cut the foolishness, see I thought I didn't deserve to be hurt. I figured the situation wasn't **big enough** for me to be hurt. It hurt that it happened to me and I held on to it because I didn't want to feel weak, guilty, or ashamed. I blamed myself for letting it happen to me. I didn't want to speak on this incident because I didn't want my family upset at me. I was afraid that I had did something bad. I couldn't tell my parents I was molested, because I thought about how it would make them look; Parents letting their own child get molested. I didn't want people judging them. They taught me all these rules and I got molested. Which made me feel even more ashamed because I knew better than to put myself in that situation. I felt horrible after it happened because I watched him entertain another girl. So, I knew more than anything that I felt used, after this molestation occurred. I was crushed. I wanted to be protected.

For you:

Reclaim your feelings and release them:

Write about anything that could be affecting you now or has affected you for a while. Whether you call it big or small, just begin to write out your thoughts about it. Reclaim your feelings and go the extra step to release them.

_____

_____

_____

_____

_____

_____

_____

_____

_____

_____

_____

_____

_____

_____

Chapter 8:
Speak

My Song: Speak – Jhenè Aiko

Your Song(s):

_____

It is good to know your strengths, weaknesses, and triggers to continue to walk in your freedom.

On my journey to becoming "100 percent me", authentically me, I learned that I was okay with never becoming 100 percent because it was an unrealistic goal. I became whole without ever making it to 100. That was my strive at trying to be strong and perfect at everything. I could never make it to '100 percent me' because I was a new person every new day that I lived. Confused? Simply put, not being perfect is PERFECT!

Like really think about it, tomorrow you will learn or hear about something that you didn't know the day before. Even down to meeting new people or seeing the "next big thing" floating around on the internet, that was something that you didn't see the day before, boom new information. From my perspective, I'm not the same person that I was yesterday.

I had to change my perspective on wanting to be perfect. The last perfect person died on the cross. This helped me accept my weaknesses throughout my journey because I kept trying to leave those parts out, trying to get rid of them. However, my weaknesses also made me whole. They are a part of who I am. I won't stand behind them anymore, that's where I messed up. I no longer used them as a stop sign that held me back from all my dreams. I had this misconception of believing that I couldn't become whole due to my weaknesses.

The more that I verbally spoke to my problems and admitted that I had trouble with this said problem, the smaller it became. I learned how to stop them from having a strong hold on me and began to speak to my issues within myself first. I put a huge emphasis on being able to rise up on the inside, before I could speak over things in my life. Hence my building stage.

This building stage was important for becoming the woman that I needed to be to walk in God's purpose for my life. But I didn't have to start off as strong as I thought. I figured I had to fight off and kill all my weaknesses before I could become a new person. But I just had to get in the position to stand, not fight. I struggled with wanting perfection and for everything to be flawless. I had to give that up and accept my situation and live in it as I grow.

SPEAK OVER YOUR WEAKNESSES

You don't need all the answers to grow. Sometimes you just need the right questions. Rebuke the spirit of weakness that you continuously fall short to and embrace them until they become strengths. The reason behind this is because God fights on our behalf, He is our strength. We have the authority to speak over our weaknesses because God gave us the authority to speak to anything that is not of Him by simply calling the name of Jesus.

Scripture Help:
Mark 3:11 NKJV

And the unclean spirits, whenever they saw him fell down before him and cried out saying, "You are the Son of God."

Philippians 2:9-11

Therefore, God exalted him to the highest place and gave him the name that is above every name, that at that name of Jesus every knee should bow, in Heaven and on Earth and under the Earth, and every tongue acknowledge that Jesus Christ is Lord, to the glory of God the Father.

Your weaknesses come around in patterns, if you're reading this the right way, you should be very familiar with my weaknesses by now.

Men were my weakness. I was so focused on finding the "right" man, because of my many encounters with the "wrong" man. I kept falling victim to my own trap. I decided I wanted to control and go after the man that I saw fit for the woman I was becoming. That just opened the door for so many more mistakes.

I barely even knew what I wanted in life, but I knew I wanted to secure a good man before all the "good" ones were gone lol.

I spoke over my weakness, eventually, but also made the choice to let go of that desire. "God, you can loosen this weakness, I'm ready for real this time. Remove it."

You have to pay attention and be careful about what you pray for. You can be asking God to strip you from certain situations and people who don't belong in your life, but simultaneously holding on to those people that God is trying to loosen you from. It is your job to let go and cut it off. It's not meant for God to handle your end of the agreement.

SURRENDER YOUR WEAKNESS

God will not provide you with more than you can bear. I could barely multi-task. My attention span was low beyond the flo'. I couldn't balance having a man, healing, pursue my relationship with God and focus on writing.

I've been down this road before and I knew where it led, brokenness. For those of you who can handle working towards your purpose and a relationship, whew-www, may God be with you. Kudos to you because men were my weakness. I knew I just had to be straight up with myself and learn to let go of the things that would get me out of focus.

I accepted the fact that I may go through some lonely nights, yet I must not waver to my fleshly desires. I knew I would be easily distracted and slowly but surely put men at the top of my priority list. My phrase became, "Until I can learn how to love God more than I love man, I will remain single." I fell short more than once, but I got back up.

GOD DEALT WITH ME.

I could tell you all how I had no other option but to be single. Either I was in tune with the spirit and cut the individual off or God took the man away. I couldn't bear the relations for long no matter how much I tried to control it on my own.

I prayed to God for confirmation before I got into anything. I promise I would get the green light, or what looked like a green light to me lol. None of them stuck for too long. I was taking the right steps, but the timing was totally off.

One thing I could say was that I no longer was scared to test the spirit to see if the confirmation was from God or something, I made up myself. **1 John 4:1-3 (NIV)** says, "Dear friends, do not believe every spirit, but test the spirits to see whether they are from God because many false prophets have gone out into the world. This is how you can recognize the spirit of God: Every spirit that acknowledges that Jesus Christ has come in the flesh is from God, but every spirit that does not acknowledge Jesus is not from God. This is the spirit of the antichrist, which you have heard is coming and even now is already in the world."

That's a real spill, okay! God will help you discern who's for you and who's not. This is why I stated that eventually I had to learn to let go of certain people. I learned my lesson through trial and error! I decided I wasn't going to go through the trouble of "gaining to lose" anymore. I tried it my way too many times. I starved my flesh and tried my best to stay out of contact with men and anything else I felt would be a distraction. Why spend time amongst the very thing you are weak to right now? We really set ourselves up lol. I acknowledged it as a weakness, but I didn't set myself up to give in to it anymore.

Imagine having a sweet tooth for red velvet cake, although you see its availability at the store, it's okay because it is at the store, but you indulge in that weakness once you buy it and invite that cake home ;)

Though the temptations were ever so present, God was not going to let them take me away from writing this book. I kept thinking that due to my procrastination and disobedience, this book would not happen, BUT this book was for His people. The men were a selfish act to please my flesh, so you know which of the two got dropped, right?! I remained single and focused on fulfilling my purpose, this book. Once my focus shifted, I wasn't in a rush to get a man anymore, my faith begun to pick back up and I knew my blessing was coming one day: no pressure.

GUARD YOUR MIND
(Triggers)

The enemy knows your weaknesses and will use them against you. You need to know something (the word) and someone (God) stronger than him to fight your battles.

Anxiety, depression, confusion, and many other related topics can create clouded areas in your mind, which then becomes things you profess with your mouth. It is imperative to guard your mind, to know how to speak your mind; because when you speak, be sure that they are your words and not the words of the enemy.

SPEAK LIFE

What comes out of your mouth is usually a representation of your thoughts. I was claiming victory. I was claiming breakthrough. I stopped claiming depression and anxiety. Then I lost a good friend, and in the blink of an eye it was all coming back. "God why am I left here? Why can't you take me? I don't want to be left in this crazy world." I got mad and sad all the time to the point that I couldn't enjoy a happy moment. Sometimes I found myself zoning out because I didn't know how to feel. I confided in my friend/sister in telling her how I felt or the lack of feeling anything…being numb. She told me it's survivor's guilt. I was about to claim depression and anxiety all over again. My mother laid hands on me and didn't let go until I broke out of the thoughts of going back into depression and anxiety. I continuously told myself that I was strong, that it's going to be okay, that I'm okay., that my friend is okay and in a good place. I cried 'til my eyes were swollen in grief which I had the right to do. I couldn't claim depression over losing him because he didn't belong to me. I was losing my faith that I was telling other people to have. I'm learning how to cope. All I can do is cry so that's what I did. In order to continue a path of healing, I had to speak life by using the "RIGHT" words even when in pain. Speaking life: I was very sad, shocked, and hurt but I am NOT depressed. I have released those thoughts. Manifest positivity in your mind and then in your words. Speak Life, SPEAK LIFE. Live free.

Tools: Eternal Sunshine mobile app

I had to learn how to guard my mind from my own thoughts, triggers, and other's words as well. I was a dreamer, when awake or asleep. I always had big dreams, and the devil always tried to attack me. He does not stop. He even started using my weaknesses in my dreams to trick me and confuse me. If I didn't know that power of God in my life, I would've fallen for it.

Scripture Help:

Philippians 4:7 NIV

*The word says do not be anxious about anything, but in every situation, by prayer and petition, with thanksgiving, present your requests to God. And the peace of God, which transcends all understanding, **will guard your hearts and minds** in Christ Jesus.*

SPEAK TO GOD

My Song: Speak to my Heart – Donnie McClurkin

After learning and participating in therapy, it became easier for me to tell my problems to God, because I had already expressed telling them to someone else.

Our problems are big and important enough for God to care about them too, and He'll show us that He is bigger than our problems.

I figured that because other people didn't want to hear about my problems, I shouldn't even try to bring them to God. I felt like He had too many serious issues to worry about rather than the little problems I was bringing to the table. I carried a lot of hurt and pain with me because whenever I tried to explain why I was hurting. My problems got pushed to the side because people were dealing with "bigger" issues. I didn't get the chance to be sad because there was always someone going through worse, so I had to "suck it up" and I suppress my emotions.

With God, I found out that He cares about my problems; therefore, I was too ecstatic to bring everything over to Him lol.

God cares about all of my problems, He told me to cast all my cares upon Him. Lay them down at His feet. I was withholding nothing. He listened even when no one else did. He didn't compare my problems to anyone else's or tell me to feel better.

Comparing my problems to others was a big issue that I had because I would think my issues were not as important and I would push my problem to the side. I didn't validate my feelings. What I found out afterwards was that little issues add up to bigger issues when unresolved. By giving it over to God, I was able to cast my cares and the pressure lifted off me. I got my strength back.

STRENGTHS

The enemy will place such an emphasis on your weaknesses and what you are lacking that at times you forget what you are really good at. COMPARISON COMES FROM THE ENEMY. Therefore, you must know your weaknesses and your strengths and focus on them so that no one can play you on either.

I am adding on to my strengths every day. I love learning and I know I can do whatever I put my mind to. I am multi-talented and the enemy hates that I know this about myself. He doesn't like when you unlock your potential. He wants to convince you to stay down and likes to emphasize that you're down when bad times hit. Remember, our mind is not a playground for the devil. As a believer, I know that bad times will come, and I'm okay with it because I know that joy comes in the morning. In God I have my faith and my strength, whom shall, I fear?

My Strengths:

Disciplined	Worshipper	Independent	Smart
Prayer	Writer	Creative	Speaker

What are your strengths?

_____

_____

_____

_____

_____

_____

SPEAK TO POUR INTO OTHERS

Once I learned how to speak up, I then poured into others and encouraged them to do the same.

I know how difficult it could be to speak up and I understand that some people do not want to share their story so openly and proudly because it gets ugly. That is okay. However, I hope that one day you may speak whether privately (with a therapist), with your inner circle, or publicly among many others. Sharing your story can help you heal and also give others who may have experienced the same hurt empowered to share their testimony. It becomes a domino effect. Speaking breaks strongholds that otherwise could have a negative outcome on your life.

SPEAK FOR YOUR FREEDOM

I spoke up because I was tired of being silent. I was quiet for too long and it was eating me up inside. It was time to speak up.

Throughout this entire book, I talk about speaking words of wisdom over my problems all the time because I had to make them smaller and my God bigger. I had to admit that whatever "it" is that I was dealing with was a valid problem. I had to be vulnerable about it. I had to elaborately discuss what happened and that what I was feeling was real. The more I tried to fake the problem and push it back, the more relevant it became. It seemed as if the more I ignored it, the bigger the problem got. Once I was able to gain strength and talk to someone about my problems, I started to recognize my own strength and using my own authority in speaking up for my freedom.

I was aggressive. I was angry. I was bitter. I was hurting, I was uneasy. I couldn't balance my emotions, I was fearful. I was double-minded. I was losing myself. I was becoming an alcoholic. I was full of lust. I was abandoned. I was a control freak. I was depressed. I had anxiety. I was sexually abused.

Then, I spoke up to free myself from hiding behind all of my pain. I spoke to release. I spoke to breathe again. I spoke to free myself. I spoke to everyone, the entire world. I didn't just pick and choose anymore. I broke out wild and rampant. I was a free butterfly, flapping her wings, and wanting others to join me!

I spoke for MY freedom; I am naked and free. Let's get naked.

EMPTY ME.

Tell God Your Secrets

Tell God Your Secrets

Chapter 9:

Obedience And Commitment

My Song: Forever – Jason Nelson

Your Song(s):

God, what do you want from me? What is it that you're pushing me to do?

"Write and tell your testimony. Give it to my people."

Obedience? Hated it. I hated listening to people. It grinded my gears. Like whom are you to be telling me what to do? I hated rules and itched to do the opposite of what someone told me to do. You know like when your parents tell you to do the dishes, so you want to do them even less just because they told you. Maybe that was just me.

If someone felt like they had power over me, I tested their patience just enough to feel like I won, but also make them feel dumb. Whatever it took to get under their skin, that's what I did! I just liked doing my own thing and not being told what to do. It took a lot for me to become submissive to God, I was the head honcho, I had to be dominant, because I didn't want people to play me anymore. I wasn't the weak one.

I had to let my guard down before God and understand that He wasn't out to hurt me.

SUBMITTING MYSELF OVER TO GOD

My Song: Falling on my Knees – William McDowell
June 18, 2019 10:04 pm.

I needed a safe space. Somewhere I could hear my thoughts and hear God as well. You guessed it, the bathroom. I went to the bathroom and locked myself in. I asked God to reveal the answer to a decision I had to make. My plan was to go into the bathroom and worship until He gave me a response. I worshipped and I invited Him in. I eventually got on my knees and submitted myself to Him. I asked God to lower me, to decrease me and increase more of Him within me.

I started to pray and give thanks. In no time I realized what the answer was, and I began to cry and break down, because I did not want to sacrifice what God was asking me to let go of.

Even though I know we shouldn't question God, I still asked Him why! "Are you sure want me to sacrifice work and school? I KNOW I didn't want it to be school because I wanted to hurry up and graduate, but God said what He said, BOTH!

Naturally, I wanted to place my goals and plans over God's, but I had already known what this would lead to, so I submitted to Him completely and did as I was told this time. I will let Him rule over me. Though it hurt because I loved school and I considered this was my ticket outtt! I placed all my faith in it. I was also thinking about what my family would say about me if I dropped out and quit my job. It just seemed so unrealistic. I cried but clearly, I became okay with choosing God's will as the best decision in the end.

I literally had to get serious about trusting Him and getting out of my own way. I HAD TO BE SUBMISSIVE AND PUT GOD ABOVE MYSELF. I fell on my knees and I bowed down.

THE POWER OF SUBMISSION

When you are on your knees in prayer, it is a physical sign of submission because of your posture. It is knowing that you don't care how you look to other people, but you are putting yourself into this humbling position and kneeling before God. You are literally in a physical state of surrender. Decreasing your body, your big head in front of God and allowing Him His rightful place above you.

Personally, this was hard for me to start doing because my heart was full of pride and control. I was fighting everything within myself to not bow down, even when the spirit was moving me. I couldn't understand why people prayed that way. I thought it was unnecessary. I thought I would look crazy so I fought the urge I felt to bow just so I could look cool in front of others.

Whether you believe it or not, one day the Holy Spirit KNOCKED me down face first and I had to learn the hard way about the power of submission. God showed me who He was. It's funny looking back now, and it felt so good laying on that floor, lol. My spiritual folks knew what was going down, haha.

OBEDIENCE

When you are obedient you can live in freedom, but it comes with safety boundaries and protection. Your obedience to God saves you from going down the wrong path and toward destruction.

I was hearing many voices on my journey; everyone had an input. However, I tried to focus on what God was telling me, while being considerate of the important people in my life. There were two sources of information that were clashing, God was telling me one thing from my future viewpoint, and others were looking at my current situation and giving me advice from that viewpoint.

A lot of people kept asking me what my plan was, this question started the first day I quit my job and stopped going to school, then when I left for Orlando and it never stopped coming. I got frustrated because I could not put my plan into words because I was literally letting God navigate me.

Scripture Help:
Deuteronomy 28: 13 NIV

The Lord will make you the head and not the tail. If you pay attention to the commands of the Lord your God that I give you this day and carefully follow them, you will always be at the top, never at the bottom.

Hebrews 12:11-13 NIV

No discipline seems pleasant at the time, but painful. Later, however, it produces a harvest of righteousness and peace for those who have been trained by it. Therefore, strengthen your feeble arms and weak knees. "Make level paths for your feet," so that the lame may not be disabled but rather healed.

I disliked the breaking and building stages that were happening in my life the most while going through my journey. However, it was through this journey that I found out that God disciplines us for our good. Now when I go through a breaking stage, I have a different response, "alright God, what's next? What are you preparing me for now?"

GOD SEARCHES FOR THE OBEDIENT ONE
Songs: I'll Be the One – Briana Babineaux and Respond – Travis Greene

Obedience went hand and hand with discipline. Discipline is defined as the practice of training people to obey rules or a code of behavior, using punishment to correct one's disobedient behavior. Discipline can be the product of obedience. Obedience is the action step that God is looking for because being obedient is your choice. God looks for the obedience before He can give you more.

Scripture Help:
Colossians 3:8-12 NIV

But now you must also rid yourselves of all such things as these: anger, rage, malice, slander, and filthy language from your lips. Do not lie to each other, since you have taken off your old self with its practices and have put on the new self, which is being renewed in knowledge in the image of its Creator. Here there is no Gentile or Jew, circumcised or uncircumcised, barbarian, Scythian, slave, or free, but Christ is all, and is in all. Therefore, as God's chosen people, holy and dearly loved clothe yourselves with compassion, kindness, humility, gentleness and patience.

Story Time

Obedience and putting on the NEW layer of clothing that God has for you.

Scripture Help:

2 Kings Chapter 2 NIV

This story is not about me, this is the story of Elijah and Elisha; learned and interpreted from a church sermon (fair warning the names can get tricky).

Elijah and Elisha paired together, were a teacher and student duo. Elisha being the student, followed his teacher, Elijah and traveled with him from city to city, to learn from him.

During this travel, Elisha was tested multiple times to see if he would still follow his teacher after hearing the talk of others (he say, she say), about how his teacher would leave him this day. He didn't entertain their comments though because he knew this information, he told them "I know, keep silent!" Nonetheless, He stayed true to following his teacher, Elijah.

The two of them, traveled from city to city, on a journey going through trials and tribulations, (you have to understand the definition of each city they traveled through) The cities played a key part to the tests that Elijah, the teacher, tested his student with. Each city represented a level up to prepare him for his future, the foreshadow of when his teacher was going to leave him. Elijah tested his student even more by asking him to stay put while he goes to another city, but Elisha continued to follow him. Then the time had come when the teacher had to leave. Yet, because of the preparations, the trials and tribulations from his journey in the previous cities, the student was now strong enough to walk without his teacher.

When Elijah (the teacher) was sent up to Heaven, Elisha had taken off his own garment and tore it into two. He then picked up the cloak that Elijah (his teacher) was wearing and used it to go back to the city that he came from and walk in his anointing. He was able to part the river with the information and items his teacher had taught him.

In life, there are pieces of information that we will take from others to add on to our own personal journey. In this story, Elisha picked up his new clothing.

The whole purpose of getting naked is to take off your old clothing, the layers that no longer belong to you and prepare for the new clothes God has designed just for you.

Do not think that you won't go back to the place that beat you down and caused you so much pain because you will. However, going through the journey of obedience to God, you will become equipped with tools and when you go back to that place, you will be dressed differently. This time they will see God's glory and anointing on your life.

STAYING OBEDIENT

Most days I felt like the blind man in John chapter 9, like, "God what have I done to receive this treatment?" It seemed like I was cursed since birth dealing with so many things, relationships, abuse, and fighting mental battles. I thought I had the worse luck!

In John 9, the disciples asked Jesus, "who sinned, this man or his parents, that he was born blind?" And Jesus replied "neither this man nor his parents sinned, but this happened so that the works of God might be displayed in him"

Sometimes you are so focused on figuring out what you have done so bad to receive a punishment. We ask God for forgiveness and mercy over and over, but God said, "you already have these things because of your obedience. Continue the fight, you are in this to show MY Glory to others." So! I just had to push through.

My friend Raheem sent me confirmation from a dream he had about me and the verse John 9:9. Though he had no idea why he was having the dream; he finally relayed the message. In this chapter Jesus heals the blind man, giving him sight again. The witnesses and people around did not think that it was the same man who was once blind and a beggar. Yet, the man answered and said, "yes, I am he." I know what others were used to seeing me as, with all my other layers packed on. But. This is the new me, a new creation.

COMMITMENT

Before, I was not as confident with what I could bring to the table. I didn't have enough faith in sticking to myself. I looked outwardly seeking for something and someone better. This represented how I felt internally. I assumed "my boyfriend" would find better so why keep them hostage and stuck with me? They deserve better. If I didn't leave the relationship, then the other result was me pushing them away. The root of the problem was my reflection of self, and everything I had been through. Everything was connected, my sexual trauma, abandonment and low self-esteem led to a need for security, never healing from these issues in addition to being cheated on in committed relationships, spiraled my commitment issues. I had to heal to learn to commit. Committing meant I had to put all my eggs in one basket, this time it was my own basket.

SELF-COMMITMENT

It took a while for me to notice that yes, there are a lot of beautiful people in the world, but what I have to offer is unique.

January 2, 2020.

God what do you think about me?

You are loving, powerful, kind. Humble, stingy, protective, a listener, hardworking, hardheaded, you love me, you're a seeker, a doer. Yet, you are gray-halfway.

Welp! Time for me to be serious and commit to myself and God.

Story Time

How can you commit to someone else when you don't know how to commit to yourself? I started things and never finished them. I had to check myself and commit to myself before anyone else. I started my year of becoming fully committed to me in June and I stopped halfway in. I started to place other people and things above myself again because it's in my nature to care for others and then I just end up forgetting about myself. I refocused and began my journey again on January 2nd. I made a vow again to keep myself first even if other people were in the picture.

I had a wild thought, what if I bought myself a ring? I bought it! Then I got even crazier. I said, what if I had my own wedding? And as crazy as it sounds, I did that too. I planned my own wedding to marry MYSELF. I bought the ring, I picked the dress, and I was about to have a whole wedding in my room. However, I had a wonderful "decorator" named Diamond step into my vision and add more to what I was trying to bring to life. We went all out at Dollar Tree (HA!) and decorated part of the house! I was sending out text invites for people to join via phone and social media. I told everyone to be there at 2pm, but it got a little shaky because it rained all day. We had a back-up plan to fix it where it could all happen in my room if necessary, but I was counting on that rain to stop. I said my prayer to God, please bring the sun out and guess what the sun came. However, yall know what they say about rain on a wedding day, right? It's good luck :).

I took it so seriously that I even had a dress rehearsal the night before. I was so excited. It may have sounded crazy to others, but I did not care.

My vows went like this:

With this ring I vow, to love you forever and then some. Through sickness and in good health. When you are low to the flo' and as high as kite. I vow to love you through the good decisions and the bad ones you've already made and the others you may make again. I promise to stick by your side, even if it's just us there together. I promise to pick you up when you're down. I promise to hug and kiss every bruise. I promise to be sensitive, but also hold you accountable.

I promise to accept you. I promise to choose you.

I promise to never leave you again.

I promise to push you to go after everything you want in life.

I promise to give you grace and forgiveness.

I promise to humble you while trying to keep you confident, bold, and free.

I promise, I promise, I PROMISE to love you forever to these things I promise,

Mrs. Tiffany B. Lockhart.

YAYYYY!! Excuse my excitement. I'm reliving the moment.

EVERLASTING COMMITMENT

God never leaves you; He is forever committed to you and His promise for you. You must continue to seek to Him, it is not a one-time thing and then you're set for life. This relationship requires your time and your commitment. Similar to a gym membership, you can have the card, but you won't see results unless you are actively working out.

God was always committed to me, and He will continue to be committed to me!

God revealed his commitment to me, when He strategically sent my little brother, Brandon. He may have been a gift for many others as well, but I can only explain how God revealed this gift to me.

It was on January 11, 2005 that my little brother was born. 1/11, for those of you who are number people and can connect and understand the visual of these numbers. For me it meant alignment. He entered this world shortly after my 8th birthday and though I told everyone how much I didn't want him when my mother was pregnant, when I saw him for the first time, that changed. I never felt alone again when he came into this world. I didn't notice how much I needed him at the time. I wanted to do everything with him and for him. I wanted to protect him. Although I was hurting during this time, from experiencing molestation and abandonment, he filled the void of my pain for a while. I never felt distant with him, I loved him unconditionally and my heart was full and wide open to him. He was always there, partly because he couldn't go anywhere, but he was definitely a bonus.

I was always given favor and protection. I am God's child; I know my identity. Thankful for your everlasting commitment.

MORE THAN PURPOSE

I was so focused and tied to walk in my purpose and write this book that I couldn't focus on what else God was trying to get from me.

I thought to myself "It's more than just purpose" and that's when I realized it's about other lives, families, and the freedom attached to this purpose. It's more than purpose strictly attached to me.

It's kingdom building, and for some reason God saw me fit to do this. It is more than wanting to finish a book or starting a business. It is a LIFESTYLE.

I ran from this kind of talk because I didn't want to be fully in, I just wanted to do the book without my face or name on it. I didn't even want to be known for it because I knew it came with other responsibilities. But God kept singing, "There is more that I require of thee" I had to make sure I knew what it meant to be committed.

Chapter *10*:
Walk In Faith, Gratitude, And Humility

My Song: Oceans (Where Feet May Fail) – Hillsong United

Your Song(s):

_____

FAITH

I have seen God do many miracles in my lifetime for others. I witnessed God do miracles for me. I had the knowledge that God could do exceedingly and abundantly, above all I could ask and hope for! But I didn't have the faith to walk with that knowledge. My problem was letting go of the old to walking into the new.

What I knew and saw in the past happened already; I SAW it. That was my evidence. Yet the future, I could not see. I straddled the fence between walking backward and forward because I could not physically see nor interpret what was coming. I loved my past despite my hardships because I was comfortable in that space. It was easy to keep going back because the future was too uncertain for me to freely walk into it. The past looked sturdy to lean on however, leaning on God was even better, my faith in him is what really helped me walk forward.

When you get a glimpse of your future and confirmations about where you are headed from God, things can start to look a little more promising. **Proverbs 29:18 NIV** states that where there is no vision, the people perish: People can perish mentally, spiritually and physically without vision of their future. God's vision for your future can provide hope, that greater is coming.

Faith is what you need to keep pushing while you wait. Although, I could not see where God was taking me, I just believed.

I made it to the end of the road where I could not see what was next anymore, AKA "where my feet failed". God's word and my faith was all I had to keep me going after God's promise for my life. When there is no one cheering in your corner 24/7, you must believe in it for yourself to keep pushing. No one can really understand your drive as hard as you can. This is something God placed in you. Knowing this, I took whatever faith I had in myself and put it in God to do whatever He called me to do and walk-in whatever direction He needed me to.

Again, I did not have any plans or goals before hand; I just kept writing. I was literally walking by faith and not by sight.

Scripture Help:

Hebrews 11:1 (NIV)

Now faith is confidence in what we hope for and assurance about what we do not see.

Hebrews 11:6 (NIV)

And without faith it is impossible to please God: because anyone who comes to him must believe that he exists and that he rewards those who earnestly seek him.

(You can read the whole chapter of Hebrews 11, and recognize the many examples of how each person's faith in God, was worth holding onto when God's promise revealed itself. It Is your faith that carries you through.)

Having faith will stretch you from comfortable to uncomfortable. I watched as God protected me from multiple car accidents, I watched Him take me through school, provide cars, food, and shelter for me. But I always got comfortable when He placed me in a good position. I didn't want to stretch to become what He created me to be.

It's a different level of faith when you know that God is going to pull through, AND you are not worried or stressed about it. We all can have faith that God will work it out, but we fail when we worry about the how. God is the chef and the best thing we can do is to stay out the kitchen.

With my strong faith, there was no more settling for less! There is no better way to increase your faith, than practicing the action! Live your life faith filled!

GRATITUDE

My Song: I Am the One - Kurt Carr

I HAVE A GRATEFUL HEART, LORD, I SAY THANK YOU!

While I was watching everyone around me prosper and enjoy life, I thought I was the one missing out on something. I was mad at God, but still appreciative for letting me live to see another day. I was bitter and envious at everyone because I was frustrated with my life. I wanted to live freely and not care about the inner work I had to do to continue to build a relationship with God. I felt trapped between living a Christian lifestyle and living with no responsibility to my purpose. Trapped living my life for others and not myself. Once you get in your lane, there is no room for you to even worry about anyone else. So, if you are feeling this way, like I was, angry, bitter, frustrated, and unhappy with your life I would suggest you go through the process of asking God for your purpose, while waiting, open your heart for gratitude in what you have right now.

GRATITUDE IS THE ATTITUDE

It was hard to not feel gratitude for all God had done for me. I felt grateful about things I would've been angry about before understanding that you must go through something to grow. I accepted my new heart of gratitude and found a way to be grateful every day. My car broke down. I was grateful I got the chance to ride in it when I did. Someone stopped talking to me. I was grateful to have them as a friend for the time being. It is what it is.

I expressed my gratitude to God in worship. I thanked Him for everything, the good and the bad. I was grateful because I knew my breakthrough was around the corner.

Scripture Help:
Luke 17:11-19 NIV

The story of ten lepers (those who have leprosy, a chronic infectious disease caused by Mycobacterium) discussed on how they were on their way to get healed and only one came back to say thank you. How many times do we take the blessing and not give thanks?

I made sure to go to God in prayer just to say thank you and not even ask for anything anymore. My prayer life became much more intimate. I knew Him and He knew me. I used this when praying for others, because some simply do not know that we can run to the father about anything. I could call on God at any time, just to commune with Him, this is where my gratitude came from.

Prayer to Express Gratitude:

God, I come before you to express my gratitude. I want to tell you thank you for being a great father. Thank you for being the same father, yesterday, today, and forever. No matter what it is that I may be going through in this moment, I know that you are always making a way on my behalf. Thank you for what you have done, doing, and going to do in my life. I expect and receive the abundance that you have for me. I will walk in your will for my life, no matter the circumstances because you know all things. Thank you.

Begin to list the things you are grateful for:

_____

_____

_____

_____

_____

_____

_____

HUMILITY

I lifted up my confidence, I found my identity. There was an increase in my mental strength. My emotional being was finally put together. An abundance of increase in my finances. My spirit was soaring high. I felt like I could do anything like I was on top of the world! I lost focus of being humble, although I know I didn't get to this place on my own, it was all God.

Somehow, I became big headed, feeling like I could demand and receive things I was not even equipped for. I KNOW that all things are possible with God, but I also believe that God prepares us in mysterious ways for what He grants you. I was telling and demanding God to give me my heart's desires more than asking may I receive all things through him. God prepared me by humbling me. He set the record straight, reminding me that I am lower than Him, and that I can do nothing without HIM. I tried so many times to get things done my own way. Yet, for the impossible to get done, I needed my trust and believe in my impossible God. I humbly stated, "God I tried it on my own and I just can't do it but God you can."

I submitted myself before God and I feared him. I learned my lesson. I am a nobody in comparison to God. This was the most important lesson I ever learned, to walk in humility.

You will not be brought up until you learn humility.

Scripture Help:

Proverbs 22:4 NIV

Humility is the fear of the Lord, its wages are riches and honor and life.

James 4:6 NIV

But he gives us more grace. That is why scripture says: "God opposes the proud but shows favor to the humble."

Luke 18:14 NIV

"I tell you that this man, rather than the other, went home justified before God. For all those who exalt themselves will be humbled, and those who humble themselves will be exalted."

*Favorite Scripture - Phil. 4:11-13 NIV

I am not saying this because I am in need, for I have learned to be content whatever the circumstances. I know what it is to be in need, and I know what it is to have plenty. I have learned the secret of being content in any and every situation, whether well fed or hungry, whether living in plenty or in want. **I can do all this through Him who gives me strength.**

CLOSING STATEMENTS:

God gave me the vision for this book. He used people to intervene in my path to speak to me and encourage me and inspire me to get it done. God knew what I needed because most of the time I just stood there with my arms crossed and a straight face telling God and everyone else, "NOPE, wrong one. I can't write." I didn't know what I would even talk about in a book that people would be interested to read. I didn't believe that anyone would want to hear about my failure with relationships, family issues, and low self-esteem problems.

My courses in life have provided me with the details that I needed to write this book and I believe that everything was purposeful and designed strategically. Although I could have struggled with remaining angry and bitter in my situations, I decided to fulfill my purpose and heal instead, to create a new me!

I am thankful for everyone who played a part in my journey, whether they knew it or not. My parents, Barry and Mary Ann Lockhart. My brothers and sisters, extended family and friends who help mold me. Lastly, specific shout out to my Broward gang, and my Orlando gang holding it down while I was writing the book.

I wrote this book to share my journey and my encounters with God. I wrote this book for whoever needs help in their faith. I wrote this book for others to speak up. I wrote this book for others to heal. I wrote this book for my own healing. I pray that you receive healing as you read. Above it all, God will get the glory.

It took a lot of time, mistakes, pressure, pushing, waiting, jumping, limping-- but it's here.

LET'S GET NAKED!